CATSONG

*Winner of the 2007 Merial Human-Animal
Bond Award*

T. J. BANKS

Published by BookLocker.com, Inc., Bradenton, Florida.

Printed in the United States of America on acid-free paper.

BookLocker.com, Inc.
2014

First Edition

For all the cats who have graced our lives – the strays and the purebreds, the soul-cats and the heart-cats, the generals and the goofballs. You all gave us so much.

AUTHOR'S NOTE

Some of the stories here were previously published in Guideposts' *Soul Mender, Their Mysterious Ways, Touched from Above,* and *So Many Miracles* as well as in *laJoie* and *Just Cats!*. Several also appeared on the following websites: www.cleverkitty.org, http://hazardcat.blogspot.com, http://consciouscat.net, and http://kimcady.blogspot.com. An excerpt from "Tikvah's Kitten" placed second in the Lynchburg (VA) Humane Society's 2005 Pre-Furred Fiction Contest

ACKNOWLEDGMENTS

As a writer, I've been blessed with editors who have also been good true friends: Nancy and Bob Hungerford of *Just Cats!;* the late Phyllis Hobe of Guideposts; Jeremy Townsend of PublishingWorks; Rita Reynolds of *laJoie;* Kim Cady, who gave me the go-ahead on "Derv & Co.," the column that became the basis for this book; and Ingrid King of The Conscious Cat.

A special thanks to Susan Graham, my agent, for her support -- and for Moonlight, my beautiful Lilac Aby girl who will be figuring in some stories of her own down the road.

Many thanks, too, to Thomas D. Morganti, DVM, who has seen us through so much, and to the entire staff of the Avon Veterinary Clinic, past and present. And no book about our cats would be complete without a special remembrance: the late Mary Ellen and Kenneth Hape of Singin' Cattery who brought so many wonderful Abys into our lives. All of you are woven into the warp and weft of these stories.

And, saving the best for last, I want to thank my son, Zeke Morris Spooner, for coming up with the Prologue's dialogue. It's funny, it's inspired, and it has the A. B. Aby Seal of Approval.

CONTENTS

Prologue

Rory – a. k. a. Aurora Borealis, a. k. a. A. B. Aby – looks up at me from the breezeway radiator, where she's baking herself. Her enormous yellow eyes are even more enormous. *Can I have a story written about me? Can I? Can I? C'mon!*

"Maybe," I tell her. She's hard to resist.

Rory ponders this. *But I broke your ankle.* She looks poutier than ever...which is no easy trick, considering that pouty is her workaday expression.

"That's not helping your case."

I'll break the other one if I don't get a story written about me. She would, too. For a long time now, I've suspected that she somehow got those long spoon-shaped paws of hers on the X-rays of the ankle that I broke trying *not* to trip over her on the cellar steps. She probably brings them out at parties to show the other cats.

"Are you resorting to threatening?" I ask.

Rory nods her Blue Aby head.

I will write about her eventually, of course. She's too much of a personality to ignore, this Rory of ours. But, then, one way or another, they all wander, paw, and miaow their way into my writing. It all started with a lanky red tabby named Alexander....

--- *T. J. Banks. Dialogue by Zeke Spooner*

CZAR-CAT

He sat on the old kitchen table, a lanky red tabby. Definitely full-grown. Like the table, he had been somebody's discard. He was nothing like the cuddly yellow kitten that my grandmother had told me to expect and everything I needed.

We looked each other over. Despite his skinniness and blatant lack of pedigree, he had an aristocratic manner. And somehow my almost 9-year-old mind got the notion that I should greet him as any cat worth his whiskers would want to be greeted. I went over to him and gently rested my cheek against him. He rubbed his face against my hair, showing me that he understood. From then on, he was my kindred spirit in a fur suit.

Of course, I already had a cat - we all had cats, most of them shanghaied from our grandparents' farm -- but Sandy was skittish, almost feral around humans. So, a few weeks earlier, my grandmother had promised me one of the kittens who were always lurking behind the hay bales in the barn. My father and I had gone up one Friday afternoon, after he got home from work, to pick the kitten up, only to find out that a cow had stepped on it, killing it instantly.

A week or so later, Dad had been rushed to the hospital with a heart attack. The next morning, Craig, Gary, and I had been left off at the farm while Mom and our older brother, Marc, had headed to the hospital. My grandmother, wanting to comfort me, had come up with the only solution she could think of: a kitten. Flipping through the local weekly paper, she'd hit on an ad for free kittens. "A yellow one or a black one?" she'd asked Craig once she'd gotten hold of the person who'd placed the ad.

"Yellow," he'd quickly replied, and Alexander came into my world.

He helped me get through the next few weeks till Dad came home from the hospital. He took to waiting with me at the bus stop in the morning. I'd pick him up, and he'd let me hold him for awhile; then, being an upwardly mobile kind of cat, Alexander would leap from my arms to the top of my head. He'd sit there, lordly in his stripes, checking out the traffic patterns, and I, little nut job that I was, would be standing by the stone lamp post in the front yard, wearing this full-grown cat like a bizarre stove-pipe hat.

When the school bus came back around in the afternoon, he'd be sitting alongside the driveway, waiting. He was the first cat who was all mine, comforting me whenever I was sick or lonely. Mirabel Cecil's book *Lottie's Cats* was light years away in my future -- I didn't happen upon it till my daughter, Marissa, was a baby -- but, like Lottie, I already knew that some cats were magical. And Alexander, in my eyes, had more magic up his paw than most.

I brought him to my school pet show, where he won a blue ribbon for "The Longest Tail." I put -- I'm ashamed to admit this now -- doll clothes on him, and he let me. I drew pictures of him and wrote stories in which he fought vampires and other beasties and things that went bump in the night. (I was a big "Dark Shadows" fan.) As he grew older and filled out, his tabby coat turned a warm golden-red, set off by his white cravat and gloves. He looked positively regal -- ergo, his new name, Czar Alexander Meshuganov. ("Dark Shadows" was going off the air by then, and I had stumbled upon a new love, history.)

He was very playful. Whenever Craig practiced his golf shots in the front yard, Alexander was there. As soon as the putter hit the ball, he'd be on it -- literally -- and Craig would be out another golf ball. He also took it upon himself to help Craig with his insect collection for science class, crunching down on grasshoppers with true gourmet gusto.

He had a sense of humor. Once, he followed my brother Gary out to the field: Gary, who happened to have some string on him, began dragging it through the grass. Alexander, of course, pounced on it. Gary began running downhill with the string (the field was anything but flat), only to realize after a few moments that the paw-tugging on the other end had stopped. He whipped around and saw Alexander sitting at the top of the slope. Just watching. *That was fun. Let's try it again, kid -- with feeling this time.*

My Czar-Cat was also a lady's man. He took off regularly to squire the various she-cats in the neighborhood around. A goodly portion of the kitten-crop at our house alone sported red tabby markings in varying degrees. One long-haired tortoiseshell kitten, Sassy, had half a red tabby face.

Once Alexander had had his pick of the females-in-residence -- the ladies found his stripes and his low-pitched melancholy miaow irresistible -- he'd vanish. Then, just as suddenly, he'd be back, climbing the screen door and crying to be let in. Or I'd wake up during the night to find him serenading me from the wall under my window.

So, when he disappeared in the early spring of my last year of junior high, I figured that he was off on another one of his rendezvous. As the days turned into week, however, I began to worry. I searched the field for weeks, then sadly faced facts. My beloved Czar-Cat was gone, taking with him all the magic he'd brought into my child's world.

Years later -- I was in college by this time -- my mother and I pulled into a parking lot and saw a red tabby moseying about. "Looks like Ali," I said, falling back on one of my nicknames for my old friend. I added jokingly, "Maybe it *is* Ali."

Mom threw me an odd look. "You don't still believe --"

"No," I replied. "He just *looks* a lot like Ali."

Then Mom blurted out the whole story. Craig had gone out one morning and found Alexander lying dead behind the tool shed. "We can't tell her," Dad had said when he'd heard the news. "It would break her little heart." So Alexander had been buried quietly behind the shed. "It was for the best," Mom assured me hastily.

"No, it wasn't," I retorted angrily, remembering the heart-sick child combing the field. "I spent *three* weeks looking for him!"

Still, the truth had, as they say, set me free: the painfulness of that long-ago but very real loss was gone now that I knew

Alexander hadn't left me willingly. That death had, in all probability, come for him quickly. He *had* seemed oddly listless for a week or so before his "disappearance," and we had never known how old he truly was.

Chemistry -- kindred spiritship -- call it what you will -- is a funny thing. There's no dictating it. Somehow two souls knit together and stay knitted together, no matter what. Even death cannot undo those ethereal skeins. Every time I see a red tabby, I remember the cat who gave himself wholeheartedly to a child. Who taught her the Importance of Speaking Cat. Those are things that have shaped me -- that I bring with me each time I let a new cat into my life.

Seems that Alexander left some of his magic behind, after all.

CHRISTY

If I look at the photo from a distance, I almost can't see her. The little Siamese cat sits sideways underneath the old dryer vent, her head slightly bent and her creamy-coffee fur almost blending in with the short brittle autumn grass. But if I look more closely, I can just make out Christy's rich Sealpoint markings and her morning-glory-blue eyes. And the rounded stump where her left front leg once was.

It's the only photo I have of her. Christy came into my life when she was a little over a month old, a gift from a college friend of my mom's. She was the runt of her litter: she never grew to full adult size, which gave her a dainty porcelain-miniature sort of look. She was, like most Siamese, both a talker and a one-cat person. She literally spent hours curled up in the crook of my arm while I read, only taking time out from her naps to punctuate a particularly tasty book page with her teeth, eat the tassel off a bookmark, or wash the insides of my ears.

Christy was about a year old when she was hit by a car in front of our house. Gary rescued her from the other side of the road where she'd been flung; then he held her while Marc drove to the vets'. When I saw her the next morning, she was lying unconscious in a cage. It was hard to believe that she had even a prayer of pulling through, but the vet on duty was more optimistic. What I didn't notice – but what my parents did – was that he kept checking her left front leg and sniffing it.

Miraculously, Christy *did* come to, and we brought her home. She returned to the veterinary clinic a short time later, though. The nerve endings in that left paw were dead, the vet told us, and it would have to be amputated before gangrene set in. He had suspected from the beginning that it would have to be done.

Mom and I went to pick Christy up the day after her surgery. We stood waiting in the examination room, too tense to talk.

Finally, the vet came in, followed by a tech carrying my little Siamese girl.

The tech put her down on the metal table. I saw the shaven neatly stitched stump where her front leg had been and swallowed hard. Christy hopped across the table to me, raised herself on her hind legs, and placed her remaining front paw on my shoulder. She gazed at me, her eyes glowing like blue star sapphires. It was a whole-box-of-Kleenex moment. I had never seen such love in an animal's face....

She became our first semi-indoor cat. Dad, who'd grown up on a farm, still had trouble with the notion of a full-time house cat; but he and Mom agreed that she couldn't live safely outside with the other cats anymore. So I set up a bed and litter box for her on the enclosed back porch, and she spent much of the day and evening in the house proper.

She learned to get around pretty well on three paws. In fact, she only limped if I brought one of the outdoor cats in for a visit. Then she'd put on a truly impressive one-cat show. *How could you do this to poor invalid me?* her blue eyes would demand. As soon as the offending cat or kitten went back outside to the tool shed, however, Christy would drop the limp and practically pirouette around the kitchen. The house was hers again. She wasn't sharing her porch privileges or our reading time with anybody, thank you very much.

Sometimes I took her outside for a little exercise. She'd explore the sideyard with its blueberry bush, giant spruce tree, and Dad's vegetable garden, while I sat and watched from my favorite spot by the lilacs. It sounds idyllic, I know, and it was up to a point. But I had to be prepared for anything with Christy. You see, she had this very real problem remembering that she was disabled whenever she went back to her old haunts.

Take Cassandra, for instance. For some reason I could never fathom, Christy hated the shy, sweet little tiger cat. Maybe it was some rivalry left over from when they'd both bunked in the tool shed together. Or maybe she just disliked other female cats on general principle. Either way, she took off after Cassandra every chance she got, chasing her down the field behind the shed... and I'd be hoofing it right behind them, trying to nab Christy before she reached the road.

Or she'd shimmy up one of the maple trees before I could stop her. She'd get as far as the lowest branch; then that right front paw would tire, and she'd start to lose her grip. Thankfully, I always managed to grab her before she fell.

Nerve-wracking? Hell, yes. And yet...there was something very sweet about those summer evenings, when this soft golden light spilled all over the yard and field and I watched her sniffing plants. I didn't know about the concept of "stop time" then. But time did stop for us, and Christy, the lilacs, the garden, and I all became one, preserved in the golden-glow as though in amber and yet wonderfully free.

A bacterial infection finally carried off my talkative, temperamental friend. We knew from the beginning that there wasn't going to be any miraculous recovery this time. Two weeks, the vet – the same man with the chiseled face and sad eyes who'd taken care of her after the accident – said, and once again, he was right. So I just spent those precious weeks sitting next to her little cat bed, stroking and talking to her. Letting her know how loved she was.

I found her there, stiff and still, one June morning and buried her under the spruce tree where she'd so often played. The pain cut too deeply for tears. Christy had given her entire Siamese heart over to me, and without her, there was only this awful emptiness.

She is still with me in so many ways. I see her delicate rounded face in photographs or drawings of other traditional or apple-head Siamese, her grace and lovableness in my half-Abyssinian cat, Zorro. And she is with me in my writing, appearing in two of my short stories – once as herself and once as a stray red tabby with the same disability. In both those stories, the cats' physical handicaps become metaphors for the heroines' sense of being emotionally crippled. Like the cats, the women in these stories learn to cope, to "move without even the shadow of a limp."

And she is in my book *Houdini*. The cat in that book has the name and face of a much loved Flamepoint Siamese – another magical cat from my childhood – but the heart and soul of the story are Christy's.

JASON

The long-haired black-and-white stray was moseying around our backyard again. I watched him from the kitchen window for a few moments. "Looks like Jason," I murmured to my husband and an old high school friend who was visiting us.

Karen came over to the window. "It does," she agreed.

Tim joined us. Despite his jokes about Jason's weight ("So, when are you going to cook that cat? Could feed a family of eight."), my husband had been very fond of him. "Just like a Stephen King novel," he remarked. He made his voice go spooky. "The same but not the same...."

Jason came to me the same day that Christy died. "You have to get another cat right away," my friend Priscilla urged me, "or you won't do it." We found him in the local flyer (the same one that my grandmother had found Alexander in and that would lead me to Derv many years later): by early evening, a kitten, all long hair and tuxedo markings, was toddling over to where I was lying on my parents' living-room carpet. He hopped up on me and stretched out full-length along my throat. I was His Now, he informed me solemnly and went to sleep. It had, after all, been a long tiring day for him.

Jason didn't give me a lot of time for grieving. He didn't fill Christy's place so much as he created one of his own. Wherever I was, he was right behind me, a tubby little black-and-white kitten with a feathery tail and a single agenda. One day, when I was heading upstairs, he decided to go for the quicker over-the-railing route. Unfortunately, he misjudged the distance and landed tail-end up in the wastebasket at the foot of the stairs. When I rescued him, he just stared at me, his yellow eyes beseeching. *You won't tell anyone about this, will you? Any other cats, I mean?*

He slept down in the cellar. I'd sit down there with him for awhile some nights, and his nightly ritual was, far as I could tell, pretty much the same: he'd carefully choose a sock from the dirty

9

laundry basket (for some reason, he preferred men's socks), then carry it in his mouth over to the clean laundry basket, hop in, and go to sleep. Apparently, the sock served as his teddy bear or security blanket. In the mornings, soon as Dad let him up from the cellar, he'd be at my bedroom door, minus the sock, and miaowing.

Jason grew into an imposing 18-pound cat with a tail like the ostrich plumes that fashionable Edwardian women used to gussy up their hats with. Unfortunately, he also picked up some issues along the way, and they weren't as funny or endearing as his nightly sock. He was the first totally indoor cat we'd ever had; and when he was a year-and-a-half-old, my parents insisted on having him declawed. To be fair, they honestly didn't know that declawing meant removing the entire last bone of each toe: none of us did.

Traumatized, Jason resorted to biting, which made his visits to the veterinary clinic horror movies complete with banshee shrieks, muzzles (which he worked off), and, once, even a restraint pole...until an older more laid-back vet finally took charge. He simply opened the cardboard carrier, flipped Jason out, did what he had to do, and flipped him back into the carrier. There wasn't even time for a good *"mer-row."* Jason had met his match.

Despite all this, Jason could be very lovable and loving. He would curl up on my stomach whenever I had cramps and turn himself into a magnificent tuxedo-style heating pad. He was less than thrilled about my going away to college. I'd start packing, and he'd jump into my suitcase. *No more room,* the yellow eyes would inform me. *Suitcase very full. Guess you'll have to stay.* I'd lift him out and put some sweaters in; he'd hop back in, and I'd pull him back out again. The whole routine would last a good half-hour before Jason lumbered off to work on a Good Sulk.

The suitcase game ended when I decided to take a year off and look for a school closer to home. In the interim, I took some women's studies courses at a local college. Every afternoon, when I got back from classes, Jason would be waiting by the cellar door, miaowing non-stop about His Day. He'd sit on my lap while I studied and Took Umbrage (he was a Very Victorian sort of cat) whenever I had to get up. I was Still His, he informed me, and I Had Better Remember That.

"Look at how he follows Tammy with his eyes," Dad would chuckle as Jason watched me head upstairs to my room.

My father had more time to notice things like that because he had just retired and retirement wasn't sitting well with him. He wasn't used to not working, and the time just hung on his hands. So he was delighted when Jason adopted him, too.

Dad had always liked animals, but I never saw him dote on one like he did on Jason. They developed their own little routines, which stayed in place even after he went back to work part-time. When Dad went upstairs to change out of his work clothes, Jason would be trotting behind him, a big furry valet; a short while later, he'd trot right back down with Dad, holding his plumy tail high. "C'mon, buddy," my father would say, patting the sofa as he lay down for his afternoon nap. Jason would hop up next to him, not leaving his side for hours. Sometimes they'd even have these playful little sparring matches.

"Stop tormenting the cat, Morris," my mother would say.

Dad, a former boxer, would grin up at her. He and his buddy understood each other. "One minute, he's makin' love to me, the next, he's bitin' my hand off."

If Mom ever had the effrontery to sit down on the sofa next to Dad, the cat would glare at her until she finally felt so uncomfortable, she got up. Jason would resume His Rightful Place, looking at Dad smugly through half-closed eyes. *Just us guys, right?*

So Jason divided his time and affections pretty much between Dad and me. After awhile, he mellowed enough to accept a few other humans: Tim, my boyfriend and a born cat lover, and my brother Craig, who was living at home, too. He was a "quality-not-quantity" kind of cat, and he liked His Inner Circle Small and Select, he informed us.

That circle got smaller one March night, when Dad suffered a cerebral hemorrhage. He was rushed to the hospital and died there five days later. Jason prowled the house, a lost soul. He'd just sit by the coffee table and stare at the place they'd shared on the sofa, his eyes huge, wistful, and searching....Or was he seeing something or someone I couldn't? I never was sure which it was, only that there was an uncanny quality to it. Gradually, however, Jason resumed his daily round. I don't think he ever forgot Dad: rather, he, like the rest of us, simply learned to live with the loss.

A few years later, Jason suddenly developed a problem with fluid on his heart. Twice, I brought him to the clinic, sure in my own heart he wouldn't make it. But Jason, like his old buddy, was a fighter – one time, he even bit through the vet's radiation glove – and pulled through both times. He spent his convalescence hogging my bed: I'd wake up half-off it, and Mr. 18-Pounder would be lying there with his head on the pillow. He also did little batting practice with my lipsticks. A retired athlete had to keep in shape, after all.

That June, Tim and I got married. Jason stayed with my mother and Craig: he was too old, everyone said, to uproot. Cricket and Kilah, two wild barn kittens, came into our lives shortly afterwards. But I tried to stop by to see Jason whenever I could. He was always Very Forgiving. He'd snuggle up against me, tuck his head in the crook of my arm, and nuzzle me like the oversized kitten he was.

Early the following November, I got a phone call that Jason was seriously ill. Mom and I rushed him to the clinic. He mewed weakly once or twice on the way over, but that was it.

The vet on duty found the tell-tale signs of kidney failure. Then she pushed back some of the black fur on his ears: the skin had gone completely yellow. Liver damage, too. At the very least, she said, he would require dialysis, and she didn't recommend it.

Jason managed to scare up a faint hiss. He'd keep on fighting, all right, but he was pitifully weak....I swallowed hard and told the vet that I guessed she'd better put him down.

I was planning to stay with him, of course, and told her so. Tearily but emphatically. But the vet just as emphatically didn't want me present. Sometimes, she explained, the animals sighed, made little noises that upset their owners, etc., etc.

I hugged my old friend gently. As I reluctantly handed him over to the vet, Jason feebly raised one of his white-gloved front paws in an attempt to cuff her. *He* wasn't going gentle into this good night or any other. It was a good way to go out. His old boxing buddy would've understood.

We brought Jason back to my mother's, and Craig buried him in the side yard, not far from Dad's overgrown garden and Christy's grave. And that night, when I came home crampy and depressed, Cricket came to me. She looked at me lovingly with wide kitten-eyes and hopped up on my lap. I was Hers Now, she informed me solemnly and went to sleep. She was stepping into the void, just as Jason had almost 11 years earlier....

Tim and Karen were heading back into the living room now. I took one last look out the kitchen window at the handsome black-and-white stray with the feathery tail and (possibly) a single agenda. I smiled wistfully, turning slowing away. The same but not the same.

MARISSA AND THE 'DATS'

My first cat was Smokey, a gray-striped kitten that I cornered in the silage shed on my grandparents' farm. I was seven and delighted: it was the first time I'd ever managed to get my hands on one of those half-wild barn cats. My brother Gary, bent on teasing me, pretended he was going to take the kitten away. I cried, screamed – and held on. Looking back, I'd say it was perfect training for being a freelance writer.

Actually, I only had Smokey for a short time. She never really got over her wildness and ran off when she was about a year old. But she was a part of my life long enough for me to get hooked on cats, and they've been showing up steadily in my life ever since. Our parents never said "No" to any animal we brought home, so Gary and I just kept dragging those cats back with us – zipped up in our jackets, in shoeboxes, and, once, in a cardboard carton on a plane coming back from Oklahoma. Some cats had a stronger hold on me than others, of course; they are still so vivid to me all these years later, it seems strange that I cannot turn around and touch them. One of them, a red tabby by the name of Alexander, even waited with me at the bus stop in the morning. In the afternoon, when I got off the bus, he'd be sitting there patiently in all his reddish-gold-striped elegance. We'd share tuna-fish sandwiches, and he figured in most of my early stories. He and the others taught me compassion – the need to see things through other-than-human eyes – and gave me their love and companionship when I was sick and lonely.

Our daughter Marissa is learning the language of cats at an even earlier age than I did. When she cried that first night after Tim and I brought her home from the hospital, the three female cats, Cricket, Kilah, and Tikvah, all hovered around her changing table, making anxious maternal cries. Afterwards, they all sat in the kitchen and miaowed back and forth about it. Here, they were convinced, was this large odd-looking kitten in distress and what were the humans doing about it? The males, Dervish and Zorro, behaved in a more traditionally "male" fashion: they got the hell out. Within a week or so, however, "Papa" Derv had re-thought his position and taken to sleeping on the rocking chair in Marissa's room. (Either he felt protective of her – he has always had a paternal streak almost as wide as he is – or he'd decided that a rocker with a cushion was too good to waste.) As time went on, he'd go so far as to let Marissa roll all over him and practically use him as a step stool. Sometimes he'd even try to squeeze his nineteen-and-a-half pounds on my lap while I was nursing her.

The other cats began to cautiously follow suit. Some of the more high-strung ones –Cricket and Tikvah, for instance – wanted a little extra reassurance; but, for the most part, they showed no jealousy of this stranger in their midst. Cricket, who has mothered everything from Derv and Zorro in their kittenhood to her toy soccer balls, began to take an interest in Marissa. She'd let Marissa pat her and even crazy kitten games outsides with her catnip toys outside the playpen to amuse her wide-eyed human charge. She would also appear out of nowhere whenever it was Marissa's bath time and supervise the whole process. Tikvah's interest was less maternal. She liked to sleep on the afghans that were piled on the bottom shelf of the changing table, and both she and Zorro constantly made off with Marissa's smaller toys. Tikvah would come to get me whenever she heard the baby cry, though.

Then Woody and Boris joined the household. Woody, alias "the cow cat" (he really does look like a Holstein), wasn't quite full-grown and tried to get in on the bath act. Cricket, however, took her duties as governess-cat very seriously and always chased him off. Boris, a battle-scarred red tabby whom we originally called "Mr. Will-Purr-for-Food," took one look at Marissa and decided that she was his ticket into the house. Almost immediately, he attached himself to her. He'd let her lie on him, squeeze him teddy-bear-style, and even pull out tufts of his fur. If he felt she was really getting out of line, he'd turn around and give Tim or me a nip. It was almost, as Tim said, as though he was saying to us, "Mind your kitten."

Marissa is almost two-years-old now. She adores her "dats" or "keddies" and runs after them eagerly, chuckling delightedly whenever she manages to touch one. Cricket has given up supervising the after-lunch baths – Marissa splashes too much now – but she and the others still watch her with curiosity. And even though her increased mobility has made them jumpy – literally -- they all have their preferred sleeping spots in her room.

Not long ago, I happened to peer into Marissa's room while she was napping and saw Boris sleeping right next to the crib. Now, Boris bears little resemblance to Alexander: he's stockier than the old czar-cat and lacks the latter's gentleman-cat-about-town elegance. But his fur is the same shade of reddish-gold, and the sight of him there brought back memories of that other tabby who was always there for another, older child. I stood in the doorway for awhile, satisfied in knowing that Marissa had, if not a czar-cat, at least a buddy who would come to mean as much to her as my old friend had meant to me.

SHADOW & SOUL

I am sitting at my word processor, staring tiredly at the lines on the screen. Words that were flame-vivid to me just a short while ago now feel lifeless. I've lost the magic, that sense of being spellbound by my fictional dream. I push my chair back and wonder why I sit in this room day after day, trying to weave all these words and images together. Then I hear a miaow and feel a paw on my shoulder. I turn my head slightly, and there is Cricket, balancing on her back paws ballerina-style on the edge of the desk behind me. She stares at me, her amber eyes large and anxious. Then she jumps from the desk, scurries over to my computer table, and makes a bold leap for kittykind onto the top of the monitor. She dangles her velvety white paws over the screen and gazes at me, purring. I'm no longer alone. I scritch her ears, play with her front paws a bit, and start typing again.

Cats and writing go together for me; both have been a part of my life as long as I can remember. Writing is a lonely, demanding business, and cats are especially good at supplying the quiet companionship – and comic relief – that we writers need so badly. All seven of our cats are curious about the word processor, but Cricket, chief editor-cat, regards it as her particular property. Back when she was a runty, big-eared grayish-brown tiger kitten, she used to make a point of sitting on my lap while I was typing, her eyes lighting up as she pressed on key after another or all of them at once. Tim and I used to joke about the book she was trying to write. I had more typos than usual in my stories and articles, but Cricket seemed satisfied with the results.

Nowadays she's mostly content to stretch out on the floor or atop the printer while I work, waiting for me to take a break and drag her long-tailed catnip critters around for her. The best editors, she clearly believes, should know enough to kick back during the creative process.

I think of her as my soul because sometimes she reads me better than I do. Cricket senses when I'm lonely or just plain having a case of writer's blues. She stays with me then, rubbing her face against mine and making little concerned noises. She'll curl up on my lap or on the table next to me, one white-gloved paw curled around my finger, and purr until my dark mood passes. At night, she snuggles up close to me, *squunking* happily. (A *squunk* is somewhere between a purr and a sigh, and it's the most contented soothing noise imaginable, especially on those nights when my chronic insomnia is winning the war.)

Cricket and Tikvah (which is Hebrew for "hope") are inseparable in my mind – partly because they look so much alike and partly because they both need so much more love and reassurance than the other cats. Cricket, the runt of the litter, has always had a strong need to be held and stroked. Tikvah, a former stray, still carries the emotional scars of that life and is easily startled or frightened. Tim calls her "a big complex with claws," and there's more than a little truth to the description.

Tikvah was living out in the field behind my parents' house with a single look-alike kitten when I first saw her. Something about this four-footed mom fending for her kitten and herself got to me: I immediately began putting food out for them. The kitten disappeared after a few months; but Tikvah kept coming around, torn between her desire for food and affection and her fear of people. After a few months, she'd let me stroke her head; if I tried to pick her up, however, she'd struggle, her double-paws flailing every which way. I learned to wait and let her come to me.

One day, about seven months after she first showed up, Tim and I caught her and brought her home with us. She was sick. Very sick. Her light-gray fur with the darker gray stripes and soft shadings of orange – kitty highlights, I suppose you could call them, scattered throughout her thick coat – was dull and lifeless. So were her large green owl eyes. She had worms, cystitis, and bronchitis so severe, it sounded like she was about to rip apart at the seams every time she coughed. She was not, Tim insisted, going to live with us: we already had three cats, and I couldn't keep giving into what he called my "Mother Teresa complex" every time a homeless feline came my way.

I made a few efforts to place her, but my heart wasn't in it. I couldn't think about letting Tikvah go to anyone else, stranger or friend, without feeling horribly guilty. In her own funny, hesitant way, she'd begun to trust me, and giving her away felt like a breaking of that trust. Then, too, Tikvah was such a nervous, defensive cat, I was afraid very few people would put up for long with the way she had was suddenly striking out with those extra claws of hers.

Long story short, she ended up staying with us. She already had me smack in the middle of her very capable double-paws, and Tim, despite all his talk, was really as much a mush about the cats as I was. So, she lucked out, as our vet, Tom, told her. Or, as Rod, an old bus-driver friend of mine, put it when I told him Tikvah's story and what her name meant, "Because she *had* hope." I started to say no, that wasn't quite it – we'd named her "Tikvah" because she'd *needed* hope – but then stopped myself. I suddenly realized that Rod was right: Tikvah had had hope come to her in the form of two offbeat cat-crazed humans who didn't know how to walk away and leave things as they were.

For her, it was like having a second chance at kittenhood. She had food and old-fashioned stand-up radiators and even a waterbed to snooze on (though even now, when there's a thunderstorm or a good fierce wuthering wind, she'll wake up out of a sound sleep, her green eyes wide with fear and remembering). She had toys, which she happily hoarded under the coffee table. She even had other cats to play with, once she felt less threatened by them. Tikvah wasn't too sure about us, however. She liked being petted, yes; but she'd also learned somewhere along the way that human hands could hurt you and was wary.

Two years and a lot of love and patience later, Tikvah has finally begun to trust us. Sometimes she still claws and nips when she really means to nuzzle or play; and she still gets frightened if we try to pick her up. But she also shadows me around the house and butts her head against my hand for attention. She has even become a snuggler – on her own terms. If I am lying quietly on the sofa under her favorite afghan, she'll hop up and stretch out alongside or on top of me. If I move even the tiniest fraction, however, she'll jump down and scurry out of the room.

If Cricket is my soul, then Tikvah is my shadow and not just because of the way she trails after me. She is my shadow-self, the one that wants to trust but that pulls back, remembering past hurts. She has taught me that trust – whether it's the trust of a human who finds it hard to let his soul-wounds heal or that of a stray cat who has never known gentleness before – comes even more slowly and silently than Carl Sandburg's cat-footed fog. That it involves holding one's self still and listening.

THE SWEETEST OF BEARS

She is our Original Settler, the Prototype, the Old Lady, and the surviving Charter Member of Ladies of the Club. She is Kilah Kitten, Ki, and the Star of Stage and Screen. But, most of all, she is Kilah Dee, the Sweetest of Bears.

Tim gave her that name. She was, from the beginning, his cat, just as her sister, Cricket, was mine. "How's my Sweetest of Bears?" he would croon to the tortoiseshell kitten with her orange Phantom mask. Of course, he also called her "a pork-bellied legislator because back then, she was a good two pounds heavier than Cricket.

We caught them in my Uncle Allan's dairy barn. Kilah was easy: the boldest of the three kittens, she made a bee-line for the meat scraps we'd put out. I caught her just as her muzzle and the meat were getting up close and personal. "A good cat-catcher," my uncle said approvingly. Then he shook his head. "You had to get the best one." We tried for Kitten No. 2, but the others had already gotten wise to us and made for the hay bales. Tim and I figured that our best bet was to head home with our captive and come back a little later when they were off their guard.

Kilah figured that *her* best bet was to hide from These Horrible Humans and dove first underneath the tiny Penguin refrigerator, then behind the stand-up radiator in the upstairs bathroom. Tim's parents, who'd come over to greet the new arrival, were treated to a glimpse of a many-colored tigery tail wrapped around the radiator coil closest to the wall. As soon as they left, Tim and I headed back up to the farm. We knew we had to come back with another kitten if we were to have even a prayer of getting this one to tame down in our lifetimes.

Tim had his heart set on the all-black fuzzball. "Tam," he called to me from the far side of the barn, "the black kitten's *adorable*." Problem was, the black kitten also had built-in Nikes on its little paw pads and dove under, over, and around hay bales faster than either Tim or Allan could put one foot in front of the other. Meanwhile, the gray-tiger runt had crept out of hiding and was getting ready to sink her baby fangs into a piece of meat that had fallen into the gutter. I glanced over at Tim and Allan, who were still doing a Keystone Kops chase after the furry little inkblot...glanced down at Ms. Runt, who clearly thought she was in Kitten Heaven with her great find and no bigger, bossier littermates nearby to swipe it out from under her...."Oh, well," I thought with a mental shrug and made a lightning grab for the unsuspecting gray-stripey girl. Not for nothing had I spent all those summers up at my grandparents' farm, chasing kittens with my brother Gary and my cousins: before she had time to hiss, the second kitten was in the box and on her way to the suburbs and a new identity as Cricket.

They spent their first 24 hours conferring and hatching escape plans behind the downstairs bathroom toilet. Cricket, hungrier for food and affection, sold out to The Enemy first: she gingerly came out into the kitchen and let us touch her. She didn't purr – oh, no, she had her principles, what barn did we think *she* had been raised in? – but she'd tolerate a few pets. A *few*, mind you. Kilah, on the other hand, continued to hiss and swear at us for quite some time. Then her feline curiosity got the better of her, and she, too, ventured out to get a better lay of the land.

For the next day or so, the sisters appeared to be taming down just fine. Then they discovered the "tunnel" between the waterbed drawers and spent an entire day there; by the time we managed to lure them out with tuna fish, they'd reverted to barncat-ism and wanted nothing to do with either of us. Every string we dangled for them was pointedly ignored; every hand stretched out toward them was spat at. Tim and I stared glumly at one another. "They hate us," he said. For two long-time cat lovers, it was a bitter moment. We sat on the floor in silence, thinking of the nice fluffy house-bred kittens we'd passed up for The Wild Sisters.

It didn't stay that way, of course: Cricket became my great good friend and Kilah, Tim's. But I can't honestly tell you how or when it changed. Still, by the time I pulled Kilah out of Tim's prized strawberry begonia near the end of August, we were pretty much a united front. Cricket would eat out of my hand, licking pudding off my fingertips: she even let me hold her like a baby when she scorched her paw pads on the stove burner or had a bad experience with a tipsy kerosene lamp, followed by an even worse (from her point of view) experience with bath water. And Tim, the mush, spent, oh, I don't remember how long walking both girls up and down the cellar stairs – they were skittish about the wide spaces between the old wooden steps – to where he'd moved their litter boxes. Eventually, he filled in those spaces, first with bubble-packing, then with pieces of drywall.

About that strawberry begonia: when I first pulled Ms. Dee out of it, it had only been slightly munched upon; there were still enough green leaves to give it that "outwardly respectable" look. But by the same time that next day, it was nothing but sticks. Knowing how proud Tim was of that begonia, I spent the rest of the afternoon trying to come up with a way to break the news to him.

"About that begonia --," I began hesitantly that evening, then stopped short.

Tim jumped into the silence. "That begonia," he declared enthusiastically, "has been with me since" – he rattled off a year, which in *my* rattled state, I didn't take note of. "That begonia has *history.*"

Oh, good, I thought: an opening. "You're right," I deadpanned. "That begonia *is* history."

He was so shocked by the devastation that Hurricane Kilah had wrought – by the utter *completeness* of it all – he hadn't a sarcastic word left in him. And, in Tim's case, that meant he was very shocked indeed.

Thus began Kilah's career as The Bad Girl. I'm not saying that Cricket didn't have a paw in some of the mischief: it's just that we never managed to catch her at it. Then, too, she had an incredibly innocent round-eyed kitten-face. Or, as Tim put it, "Cricket's like" – here, he pulled an exaggeratedly sweet, angelic voice out of his bag of many voices – "'Hi, my name is Cricket,' whereas Kilah's got this black mark on her lower lip that makes it look like she's got a cigarette hanging out of her mouth, and she's there" – he pulled out another voice, a tough street-chick one this time – "'Yeah, I'm Kilah – what's it to ya?'"

Whatever the real story, it was always Kilah I caught clawing the loveseat or the good blue chair. And, worse yet, whenever I yelled at her to stop, she'd just kind of slew around and throw this *look* my way, her claws still enmeshed in the upholstery. *Excuse me,* the large green eyes remarked. *You talkin' to me?* Her brazenness – her sheer kitty *chutzpah* – was such, she'd even sit next to me later on while I cobbled the fabric together as best I could. But it wasn't just *chutzpah*. No, Tim and I always swore that she was checking out my work so that she could rip those stitches again later out in less time.

Then there was the matter of that small light over the refrigerator: it was one of those old pull-chain fixtures, and I used to leave it on for Tim the nights he worked late. I started noticing that it was still on in the morning and finally spoke to Tim about it. "I *did* turn it off," he insisted. But he couldn't explain how the light always happened to be on the next morning.

A few days later, however, the answer materialized. I happened to walk into the kitchen and saw Kilah sitting on top of the fridge, angling for the pull-chain. Finally, she caught it and with one good *yank!* turned it on. Satisfied with her work, she leaped down from the refrigerator and went on to other things – terrorizing the surviving houseplants, probably. (That was the year she declared war on the jades – which is why all our houseplants now hang from the ceiling, whether or not God intended them to.)

I told Tim about my discovery that night. "Now," I said half-exasperatedly, half-amusedly, "if only she'd learn to turn it off."

"She could if she wanted to," he retorted proudly.

Kilah was also a hardened catnip abuser. Whereas Cricket could get giddy-pawed barely sniffing it, her sister could toss the herb down with the best of 'em. She was always more of a hellion afterwards, leaping up and clawing innocent hands the instant they touched the stair railings. Of course, she was very big on hands, anyway, and always believed in going for the hand dangling the catnip toy instead of the toy itself. This, Tim claimed, was a sign of her Superior Intelligence: "She knows that if you stop the hand, you stop the toy, too."

But, then, he was like that about his Kilah. Years later, when we were waiting in one of the examination rooms at the veterinary clinic, Tim began to go on and on about how much slimmer she was than her formerly runty sister. Cricket had, in fact, begun to put on weight; but, as I pointed out to him, she had a much smaller frame than Kilah, so the extra pounds had nowhere to go. The tech, who had just weighed the girls, agreed with me and left. Tim, eager to prove both of us wrong, tried to sneak Kilah on the scale while Dr. Feibel's back was turned: he didn't manage to get her squarely on it, though, and both she and the scale came crashing down. I explained to the vet what my husband had been trying to prove; and the older man looked at us as though we were a pair of nice, friendly lunatics and the cats had more brains between them than we could ever hope to have. "I would've thought she was the bigger one," he said politely, glancing toward Ms. Dee. I shot Tim a smugly triumphant look.

The sisters' first couple of years passed relatively uneventfully. We took in a couple of cat boarders – first Sparky, then Buddy – for friends on a temporary basis. The girls were not thrilled by their guests; but instead of going after the intruders as a united front, they'd start squabbling with each other.

It's your fault.

No, it's your fault – they wouldn't be here if you hadn't knocked over that jade plant and then dug it up by the roots.

Well, it was asking for it. Anyway, you were the one who stole the hair-trap from the tub and left it and all that shredded tissue around the woman while she was napping.

Hey, it's not like I was going to light a match to the tissue. I just wanted her to get up and brush me some more....

Eventually, they'd settle back down and go about their business, tolerating, if not loving, the boarders. Eleven-year-old Sparky, on the other hand, fell in love for the first, last, and only time in his life when confronted with Kilah's tortoiseshell charms and trailed her devotedly during his stay.

The two-cats-in-the-yard (or, rather, -in-the-house) equation was a good one and lasted for quite awhile. Then Dervish, Tikvah, and Zorro joined us; and in 1992, after we decided we'd had enough practice on cats, we had our daughter Marissa. The gang showed no jealousy over the baby. In fact, as Tim wrote in the baby book, she was "crying so hard" that first night home from the hospital "that all the female cats – Kilah, Tikvah, and Cricket – started crying with you. It was really funny to see the cats so worried about our new kitten."

There was a cat moratorium of about eight months after Marissa's birth. Then Tim -- who'd been going around vehemently insisting, "We are NOT taking in any more cats" -- adopted Woody, a handsome young black-and-white stray who'd been sweet-talking him out in the garden, and Boris, an older tattered-eared, down-on-his-luck red tabby, adopted us. The sisters had mellowed considerably since the Sparky-and-Buddy days (Kilah had pretty much given up the catnip) and took it all in their tigery stride. Cricket ruled quietly but firmly from her office atop the cellar cupboards, the able- and double-pawed Tikvah supplying police force when necessary.

Kilah was involved in affairs of state, too, naturally, but not to the extent that the other Ladies of the Club were. "It's Kilahdeelian quality-of-life issue," Tim would say with mock solemnity; and "Kilahdeelian" really did seem to describe the slightly detached, philosophical attitude that she adopted as she matured and left her bad-girl image behind her. Of course, she could and did still wreak havoc on unsuspecting plants. Once, I saw her wake up from a sound sleep in the third-floor office and glide all the way down the stairs. There was a shout from Tim on the first floor: when I got down there, he was trying to defend one of his sea onions with its long trailing leaves from the Wrath of

Kilah. He had taken the plant down while he was removing what he called "the garbage-bag-brown paint" that earlier owners had inflicted upon the kitchen, and somehow Kilah *knew*, even in her sleep, that there was an unprotected plant there for the taking. Strange but true.

Between Marissa and our furry Gang of Seven, Tim's work and various projects, and my writing, our world was moving along very nicely, thank you. And then that world spun off its axis. On the evening of July 11, 1995, Tim was killed instantly when his company van hydroplaned and hit a telephone pole on its way home. The weeks and months that followed are still too painful to look back on for long: it was then that I learned that grief can imprint itself on your body, lodging there like a parasite so that long after the initial trauma has passed, some totally unrelated event can set it off again. An emotional Star 69, if you will.

Marissa was three-and-a-half, too young to understand most of what was going on. After the graveside service, she could only prattle about all the "chairs. And there was a chest. The chest went down." But Kilah surprised me by acting as though nothing had changed. Remembering how Tim had loved her – remembering how Jason had acted after my dad's death -- I just didn't get it. But Kilah did. Some essential part of Tim -- call it his spirit, his ghost, his energy – lingered in the house like a benediction, and she knew it. Just like she'd known about that plant years earlier.

But, cat or human, each loss hits us differently. When Cricket died two years later, I watched Kilah withdraw into herself. She didn't do any kitty banshee wails or go searching for Cricket any more than she had for Tim. But it was clear that this loss was too much for her to bear. Maybe Cricket's spirit had moved on more quickly than Tim's: after all, she had died after four months of kidney disease, not suddenly and violently as he had. Or maybe the sisters had just been so close, losing her had been like losing a paw for Kilah. All I knew was that looking into those huge green eyes, I saw a soul as bereft as mine.

It was a kitten – a big-eyed blue dilute tortoiseshell who bore no resemblance to Cricket except for her plushiness and an endearing little lopsided white splotch on the left side of her chin – who brought Kilah out of the wasteland. Keisha is much less shy than Cricket was; but, otherwise, her personality is uncannily similar. The other cats picked up on those similarities immediately, and even Tikvah, who had loved Cricket deeply, gave the newcomer her double-pawed seal of approval...something that she gave to precious few other felines. But what happened between Keisha and Kilah was as moving as any James Herriot story.

The kitten went instinctively to the 11-year-old tortoiseshell – walked through the walls of grief, so to speak – and claimed her as a sort of surrogate mother. And Kilah, who'd never mothered a kit of her own, took her in. Perhaps Keisha touched some latent maternal instinct. Or perhaps she, like the other cats-in-residence, simply recognized another soul cut from the same plushy cloth as her beloved sister.

Whatever the reason, they were almost always together after that, the younger cat resting her head on Kilah's back or butt, whichever happened to be more convenient. And Kilah would let her. I'd come across them napping together like that on the kitchen radiator or counter, just like the two sisters used to. Sometimes Kilah would glance up at me, her eyes gentle: *I don't hurt anymore. She's not Cricket – I know that—but she's pretty good, you know?*

Three years later, they're still paw-in-paw with one another. I take my earlier words back: it's a much more moving story than any Herriot, with all his skill and all his feeling for animals, ever wrote. To me, at least. You see, I saw it all unfold right before my own eyes – proof positive that sometimes another soul can reach out to ours, past the grieving, and bring us safely back to shore.

It is, after all, as my Tim would say, a Kilahdeelian quality-of-life issue.

THE BEST BET

"Huh, she turned out better'n I expected," my uncle said, studying the full-grown gray tiger cat by the open cellar door. "I never thought that gray one would amount to much."

Tim and I had snagged Cricket and her sister Kilah from my uncle's dairy barn not quite a year before. Cricket had been the runt of the litter, a skinny boat-eared bundle of stripes who'd crept out from behind the hay bales only after we'd made off with her showier and bolder sister. Despite her shyness, however, she'd come around before Kilah. Perhaps it was, as Tim said, because she had such a deep need to be touched and held.

She became my cat, snuggling next to me while I read or sitting on my lap while I typed. Especially the latter. Cricket fell in love with my typewriter, her green eyes turning suddenly and inexplicably amber at the rapid rise and fall of the keys. Eventually, she took to *thwapping* the keys with her paws as the spirit moved her, adding a few unexpected characters to my stories. And when the creative muse deserted both of us, we'd hang out on the stairs together in companionable silence. I used to joke that Cricket was my first-born; and I certainly lavished as much care on her as any mother does on her child. Kilah got her share, make no mistake about it. But it was Cricket whom I coddle, hand-fed, frantically phoned my vet about, and played twig-catch and other games with. She would go to very few other people, often hiding atop the cupboards in the cellar when strangers came by and not re-emerging till they'd gone.

We became best buddies. Even when I started using a word processor and she no longer actively contributed to my stories, she'd lounge by my feet, playing with a catnip critter. Or she'd drape herself over the monitor, her elegant snow-white paws dangling over the screen. She was a sympathetic listener and, as I've written elsewhere, could read me better than I could read myself. She'd follow me all over the house, nuzzling and rubbing up against me anxiously. I'd start wondering what was getting her, and then *click!* I'd realize it wasn't what was getting her: it was what was getting *me*, and she with that feline sixth sense of hers had picked up on it.

We all have our faults, of course...those little smudges on our personalities that keep us from being *too* good...and Cricket's was her vanity. She'd always gloried so much in being brushed that Tim and I used to joke she should have a standing weekly appointment at the hairdresser's. The cat brush was her personal property, and she insisted on being brushed first -- the other cats had to wait their turns – and last.

One morning, I was in a hurry and brushed Kilah first. Well, Cricket had the tantrum to end all tantrums. She sat there, miaowing her head off, until her poor sister looked horribly guilty. Zorro went up to soothe his foster mother. Cricket wasn't having any of it. She kept on complaining until Tikvah decided to step in.

Now, Tikvah, crusty character that she was, loved Cricket. She went up and nuzzled her friend. But Cricket wasn't ready to stop ranting yet. Tikvah sat there and mulled the situation over. Then she went over and slapped said friend in the face: *Get over it, dammit!* And Cricket did.

Tim laughed when I told him the story that afternoon, then remarked, "Tikvah's like, 'I'm trying to be nice about this, but --!'" And he mimicked Tikvah slugging her buddy with one of those over-sized mitts of hers.

Cricket and I grew closer over the years. I had a slew of nicknames for her. Secret names. One of them was "Little Bit," a name my vet, Tom, gave her back in her runty days. Even when she grew up big – sometimes too big, as Tom would sternly inform me – and beautiful, the name clung, although it eventually underwent a sea change and became "The Best Bet." She was with me through the best of times and the worst of times. When Tim called me on the day that we were bringing our daughter Marissa home from the hospital, he went so far as to put Cricket on the phone: her rich coffee-perking-in-the-morning purr was a balm to a tired new mother recovering from an emergency C-section. And when Tim was killed in a freak accident a few years later, it was Cricket who quietly and gently brought me back to the land of the living when no human could have possibly reached me.

Early this past spring, Tom noticed that Cricket's kidney values were drastically off. We changed her diet, and she seemed to perk up, coming upstairs again, something she hadn't done in months. So I began to push my fear away…to let myself believe again that my best beloved, my kindred spirit in stripes would be communing on the stairs with me for years to come.

Then, on the second anniversary of Tim's death, I brought her to the veterinary clinic for her monthly weigh-in. She was still a big girl, but she'd lost a noticeable amount of weight.

"She looks fine," my friend Cel tried to reassure me when she stopped by that evening. She stroked the brownish-gray fur with the reddish undertones that had gradually deepened and changed its hue over the years. "Her coat feels good." Cel smiled. "She looks like she should be sitting on top of a mountain and little kittens should be climbing up to ask her the meaning of life."

By the next morning, however, Cricket had gone from being the Buddha-Cat to just being plain sick. She threw up on her front paw and couldn't summon up enough strength to clean till later in the day. And even then, she couldn't scrub it to its usual snowy whiteness. She kept to the downstairs bathroom and didn't even hiss or growl when Star, the Siamese upstart whom she loathed, tried to barge in. She wouldn't eat or drink. I gave her water through an eye dropper; smeared malt-flavored hairball remedy on her gums (OK, it wasn't food, but it was *something*); made an appointment for Monday, when the clinic would open again; and prayed.

It didn't take Tom long to size up the situation. "I think she's getting ready to close up shop," he said gently, adding that he hadn't really expected her to hold out this long. He looked at Marissa and me. "I'll give you some time alone."

I tried to explain to five-year-old Marissa what was happening so that she wouldn't be frightened. Then I laid my cheek against that beautiful velveteen coat for the last time and whispered all her secret names to her, letting her go. And I kept my hands on her as Tom gave her that last shot and she made her way out of this world, leaving behind a beloved but empty shell.

I buried her in the garden. With her hairbrush, of course.

I have two books about animals as teachers and healers lying right beside me now – books that I'm looking forward to reading and learning from. But Cricket taught me more than any book ever could. From her I learned that a cat can give you more love and understanding than I once would've dreamed possible. And that given that same love and understanding in return, a shy gray-striped runt with sailboat ears that nobody thinks will amount to much can become The Best Bet.

KEISHA

She was sitting on top of the cat tree by the pet shop door when we came in, looking for the entire world like she'd been waiting for us. *Got my bags packed*, the blue tortoiseshell kitten announced as she hooked me in with her velvety white paw. *What took you so long?*

I, in turn, was entranced. *God, she looks like Dimity!* I thought, reaching out a paw of my own to stroke the orange-flecked blue-gray fur and remembering the shy rag-bag tortoiseshell from my childhood whom I'd chosen over her livelier littermate because...well she'd needed me.

We didn't really need another cat in the here and now: we had nine, which was certainly put us past the "gentle sufficiency" point. But the resemblance to my long-lost Dimity was uncanny...and there was that huge hole in our hearts from the death of our beloved Cricket a few weeks earlier....On second thought, maybe we *did* need her, and she with that even more uncanny intuitive ability of hers knew it before we did.

So Keisha came home with Marissa and me. Discounted by the pet-store manager – she was 10-weeks-old, and most folks wanted younger kittens – she fit so easily into our household. The rest of the gang accepted her with barely a hiss (and that hiss came from Star, the Sealpoint Siamese who resented most of her species on general principle), Bandit, the gorgeous black half-Persian who was a few months her senior, became inseparable from her, so deeply did he fall in love with her.

But, then, most people were almost as smitten with Keisha as he was. Aside from her wonderful lush coat-of-many-colors and appealing expression, she had an incredibly sweet personality. And she was a born nurturer. A Florence Nightingale in a fur suit.

When she was about two-years-old, we had a series of very sweet very sickly Siamese kittens pass briefly through our lives, bringing a world of love and pain with them. All of them – the two

Houdinis and Crystal – had congenital problems: two had to be euthanized, and one, Houdini III, died in his sleep. But to watch Keisha with these blue-eyed waifs was a lesson in caring and compassion. She showed a matter-of-fact earth-motherly kindness to each of them, playing with them when they were up for it and just letting them snuggle up against her plushiness when they weren't.

With Houdini II – who was with us for only 11 days before his chronically impacted bowels made it clear that euthanasia was the kindest gift we could give him – she was especially gentle. The other cats, sensing that there was something radically wrong with this kitten, kept their distance. Not Keisha. She let the little guy huddle next to her and soak in as much of her body warmth as he could. And he would turn his triangular scrap of a face with its red-gold smudges toward her like she was the Great Cat Sun-Goddess and he was an especially grateful flower. *You're so pretty,* his wistful blue eyes said adoringly. *Thank you for being nice to me.*

So strong was this caretaker side of Keisha's personality – so big and beautiful and vibrant was she – I couldn't imagine her ever being ill or immobilized. I mean, she was always the healer, never the one who needed healing. So, when I found her lying horribly still out in the narrow cat-enclosure tunnel one early September day, my mind screamed out in disbelief.

I was horribly sure she was dead, so still was she lying. Numb with grief, I went inside to get a tool to cut through the chicken wire: when I came back, I saw that her sides were moving. Not much but enough that I could let myself breathe again. *It's just the heat,* I quickly reassured myself. *She'll be fine once it cools down.*

But that next morning, Keisha was lying flat-out in the enclosure again, worse than before. Marissa went into the large walk-in section and, crawling through the narrow cat tunnel, lifted her up onto the platform by the front-porch window. We rushed her to the veterinary clinic. Kilah, one of our older cats and Keisha's surrogate mom, seemed a little wobbly on her paws, too, so we brought her along with us.

Tom examined both cats carefully. It was, he told us, "some kind of hot corona virus." Kilah could go home with us, but there was no question of Keisha leaving. She was running a brutally high temperature and was heavily jaundiced, to boot. There was no telling how much actual damage had been done to her liver: the good news was, as Tom pointed out, we were talking about the one organ that could regenerate itself. It wasn't much to hold on to, but it was all we had.

By the next day, Dervish, "the big orange-and-white guy," and Bandit had come down with the same virus. The tests ruled out The Three F's – feline leukemia, FIP, and FIV – which made it all the more puzzling. The other cats threw off the virus quickly; but Keisha stayed on at the clinic, attached to an I.V., fighting for all she was worth. She came home the day after Labor Day: the jaundice was still there, but not as severe, and her temperature had let up a little. It could still go either way, though. I had to feed her through a syringe seven to eight times a day and somehow get the Clavamox and her other meds down her as well.

"If anyone can pull her through this," Tom said, "you can."

Problem was, I didn't feel as confident of my abilities as he did. In the last year-and-half, we'd lost a number of cats, not just Keisha's little Siamese waifs; and all those deaths had, as someone phrased it, put my "heart in a pendulous place." An afraid-to-hope locked-in-limbo place, which is one of the closest things to hell on earth I've ever known.

I did everything I could think of, even clipping a little cat guardian-angel charm to Keisha's elegant purple collar. Couldn't hurt, I figured. Didn't seem to help much either, however. She was still very weak, still very far from turning that invisible corner. I couldn't bear the thought of her dying. Finally, I sat down with her one night and, placing my hands on her, did some very basic Reiki on her.

Then it happened.

An incredible current of energy shot through my fingertips and into Keisha's plushy blue tortoiseshell fur. It was like nothing I had ever experienced before. Something – or, rather, Someone – was working through me. Like Emily Dickinson's afterlife, it was as "invisible as music, positive as sound."

Shortly afterwards, Keisha bit her feeding syringe in half. *Get that damned thing outta here,* she informed me, her pale-green eyes blazing. And by the end of the month, her blood work came back normal. She'd fought the good fight and won.

Sometimes...when you're in a betwixt-and-between place, as Keisha undoubtedly was that night...when medicine has done all that it can...Reiki/prayer and the sense that someone loves you very much and is pulling for you with every fiber of his/her being can tip the scales. I know that I felt that current, and I believe that Keisha, sick as she was, felt it, too.

By the way, she still wears the cat-angel charm on her collar, right over her name tag. Just a little reminder that faith...like 10-week-old kittens...shouldn't be discounted.

STAR POWER

Let's face it: Siamese cats, like the rich, are different. They're noisy, demanding egos in exotic fur suits. If they can come up with a way to make you crazy, they will; and, what's more, they'll patent it. Doreen Tovey, who wrote a whole slew of vivid, humorous books about her life with a succession of Siamese autocrats, summed up the relationship between Siamese and their humans like this: "People who don't have Siamese don't understand that the only way to live with one is to accede to its idiosyncrasies: they think the owners, not the cats, are odd."

Tovey would have understood about Star.

Star came to us when she was about two-months-old. She had the sweetest deep-blue eyes – hence her full name, "Starfire," short for the star sapphire they resembled – and that's about as far as the sweetness went. She never played the part of the shy, shrinking kitten around the older cats-in-residence. No, General Sherman marching through Georgia during the Civil War was more her style, and the Ladies of the Club – Cricket, Kilah, and Tikvah – eyed her askance. *Very* askance. In her first year with us, she broke countless ornaments (she had a genius for picking off the ones with the most sentimental value); nursed off Woody, our black-and-white male cat; decided that human legs made for great scratching posts; and took over Marissa's dollhouse. "Mom! Look what Star's doing to my dollhouse!" my pre-schooler would shriek indignantly.

Some things – nursing off Woody or rampaging through the dollhouse, for instance – Star abandoned along the way to cathood. But she added to her repertoire jumping on the shoulders or backs of unsuspecting guests; disrupting board games; and leaping up onto the ceiling beams and miaowing woefully to be rescued, even though she knew perfectly well how to get down by herself. She flirted with workmen and was even offered a new home by one who had a weakness for Siamese.

She staged flamboyant escapes, once making it as far as the porch roof. Another time, I was just unloading groceries from the car when Star came sauntering around the back-porch steps, nattering about The Lovely Walk She'd Had. She had, quick investigation revealed, practically turned herself two-dimensional and slid out through a narrow space in the cat enclosure. What was more, she had somehow persuaded Merlyn to join her in this Great Escape – although Merlyn, being Merlyn, was clinging to the cat-enclosure roof and crying about Missing Her Food Dish and how Tikvah had Been Right about Not Listening to Those Siamese Foreigners....

This troubled Star not at all. She clearly believed – and still believes – the old legend that Siamese cats are the reincarnations of the queens and kings of that land. Translated: she could do as she damned well pleased.

She ate Marissa's first fish, Blue, conning Merlyn into taking the fall for her. Merlyn – she was very trusting in those days – was found alongside Blue's overturned plastic tank, looking miserably guilty while Madame sat smugly nearby, having what was clearly an after-dinner scrub. Star didn't stop there. She took to jumping kittens coming out of the litter box until Bandit the Good put a stop to that by jumping *her* when *she* came out of the box. She hated Keisha – the feeling was very warmly reciprocated – and deliberately peed in a cat bed that the blue tortoiseshell was fond of. *Liked that bed, did you?* Star smirked, waving her tail triumphantly as she sashayed off.

She stole jewelry. One morning, I caught Star dragging Marissa's good watch down the stairs. Since several other pieces of jewelry were missing at that time, I speculated that she must have a stash somewhere.

"Give her a cheap plastic watch and see where she goes," my father-in-law, Bob, suggested with amusement.

"Star wouldn't take a cheap watch," I replied, and it was true.

She made for good stories. One friend told me about her ex-boyfriend's ferrets, who were always stealing socks; and we came up with this scenario in which Star ran a pawnshop (this was around the time of the jewelry heists) and the ferrets were desperately trying to get money for the socks from her, insisting that they (the socks) were "brand-new and freshly washed, too." Another friend had a little tortie cat named Flatty Bones with a suspiciously Siamese-sounding miaow: we had a running dialogue for years about how Star was sending Flatty self-empowerment tapes and trying to help her bring out "her inner Siamese." I even put Star in my time-travel novel *Souleiado,* figuring that if any cat would travel through time, it would be a Siamese.

All of this just goes to show that Star is so out there, almost anything about her sounds believable. Star running a pawnshop? Sure. Star leading Siamese consciousness-raising meetings and selling self-empowerment tapes? Absolutely.

As for her being able to stroll through time...well, maybe that *is* a little over the top. Then, again, maybe not. Siamese are, after all, different.

MANEKI-TIKVAH

At the temple of Gotukuji in Tokyo, says Fernand Mery in his book *The Life, History and Magic of the Cat,* there are statues of Maneki-Neko, the Beckoning Cat, greeting you at almost every turn. Which is, after all, appropriate since there's cat cemetery on the grounds, too. But these are not somber kitty-wraiths. No, these are friendly guardians, each with a front paw raised in greeting...each a representation of the legendary "small female cat who lures and enchants people, bring[ing] happiness and good luck."

When I first knew Tikvah -- way back when she was just a stray roaming the field behind Mom's house, with a dead mouse or two stashed in the old tool shed -- I used to see her sitting in the yard with her front paw raised just like that. Looking for all the world like she was checking for rain. Which she probably was. Tikvah was a pragmatist, a down-on-her-luck polydactyl who had known a world of suffering.

Not that she could tell us about it, of course. But after she came to live with us, we'd notice "little" tell-tale signs...such as her absolute I'm-digging-my-claws-in-and-taking-you-with-me-sucker terror at being picked up. (A lot of my sundresses had some really nice hand-embroidered flowers over the bodices to camouflage the damage she did. "Designs by Tikvah" we used to call the results.) Or the way she'd bolt from her favorite radiator perch whenever she saw me pull the broom out of the closet. Tim and I didn't want to know what had been done to her with a broom; but he muttered a few comments about what should be done to the so-called human(s) who'd abused her, and I tried not to bring the broom out when she was around. She was, as Tim used to say, "a big complex with claws."

She was also an extremely opinionated cat who made a point of airing said opinionations (my word) whenever possible. And that led to another Tim-ism: "Tik-Talk." "O. K., now, it's time for

'Tik-Talk,'" he'd announce, using a special voice he'd created just for her. It was kind of a George Bush-Meets-the-Wicked-Witch-of-the-West voice, which sounds bizarre, I know, but it utterly suited her. In fact, if Tikvah *could've* spoken, I wouldn't have been at all surprised if she would've come out with that very voice.

As far as the other cats were concerned, Tikvah was strong medicine. *Very* strong medicine. Her distrust extended to her own species. In all her years with us, she only loved one of her fellow felines: Cricket, who resembled her enough in both looks and personality that Tikvah clearly regarded her as a soul sister. She viewed everybody else with her usual double-pawed ambivalence, and that meant she had to hit them. You know – get them before they got her. *It's just on general principle,* she seemed to be saying. The other cats understood only too well.

Of course, in the beginning, we had to scold her for her unprovoked attacks on her own species. Tikvah would look at us gravely out of those pale-green owl eyes of hers – you could almost see her nodding – and bide her time. The moment that Dervish or Kilah was getting reamed out for clawing the furniture, Officer Tikvah would materialize out of nowhere and begin whacking the kitty crap out of them.

There were a couple of variations on this particular theme, and one of them had to do with the fact that Tikvah did not like being caught being nice. Sometimes during that first year, I'd look up from the book I was reading and see her surreptitiously washing the top of Kilah's head while the latter was sleeping. The instant Tikvah felt my eye upon her, she'd get flustered and start smacking the other cat alongside the head. Poor Kilah would wake up looking very dazed, very confused while her assailant glared at me. *That didn't mean anything,* Tikvah would assure me and hop off the bed.

What didn't mean anything? Kilah would want to know, shaking her head and looking like a hit-and-run victim – which was, when you got right down to it, essentially what she was.

"Never mind," I'd say, patting her. "Go back to sleep."

The second variation occurred only once that I knew of, and it involved Dervish and Tikvah's ovaries. Or, rather, a particle of one of her ovaries. You see, she'd been in heat when we'd had her spayed; and because of the swelling (we'd thought she'd been pregnant at the time), a piece of an ovary about the size of my little fingernail had gotten left in the works, sending her back into heat off and on. Tikvah had to be – I kid you not – re-spayed. In order not to do a *déjà vu* number here, however, we had to wait till the heat and Tikvah were at their worst. This meant a lot of rolling and writhing on our usually no-nonsense girl's part. At one point, she actually propositioned Derv on the kitchen table, not realizing, or caring, that he had been neutered at an extremely early age.

Derv watched her r&w maneuvers with raised eyebrows – well, with slightly curved orange stripes over his eyes that *looked* like raised eyebrows. Finally, in anger and desperation, Tikvah rose to her paws and swatted the poor guy full in the face. *What good are you?* her eyes scathingly demanded, as she did a haughty exit, stage right, from the table.

Ergo, my nicknames for her – "Iron-Paws" and "Butt-a-bingster." The latter had its origins with Pam, a half-Italian half-Jewish girl I'd known in college who had used her hands so fully, so vividly in conversation, it had been a trip just to *watch* her talk. "So I slapped him – *butt-a-bing!*" she'd say, hands flying back and forth as they underscored the action in her story. Somehow I had a feeling that Tikvah would've found Pam a soul sister, too.

Tim – who, along with his gift for mimicry, bad jokes, and worse puns, also had a talent for making up bizarre or offbeat lyrics to songs just like that – *snap!* – had to take it a step further, of course. He gave Tikvah and her significant paws their very own theme song:

> "*I am Tikvah, hear me roar,*
> *With paws too big to ignore....*"

If Cricket was the only other cat Tikvah ever allowed herself to feel close to, then I was her sole human *compadre*. We understood each other. I didn't find loving and trusting easy things to do either; just as my Butt-a-bingster had to stand up prairie-dog-style, trying to determine whether she could make the jump onto that tall bureau or that really high shelf, I had to sit back and gauge situations before making my leaps of faith.

So I never swooped down on her and scooped her up in my arms -- unless, of course, she was due at the vets' for shots. "She really doesn't like being picked up," I'd caution cat-loving guests intent on making friends with my big-pawed girl. Usually, they'd ignore me and end up finding out the truth of what I was saying the hard, scratchy way. You had to let Tikvah come to you. Her terms, not yours. Since I understood that – and she understood that I understood that – she would follow me around and burble for me like she would for nobody else.

We lost Tim and Cricket within two years of each other. With Cricket's death, there was an important shift in my relationship with Tikvah. While Kilah, Cricket's sister, became the gang's constitutional monarch, Tikvah took her old friend's place as my right-paw girl, my No. 1 familiar. She had a different way of showing her love than Cricket had had, but it held just as strong and true, even in that last year, when arthritis slowed her down drastically.

Slowed her down, yes, but it didn't stop her completely. Not, as old Iron-Paws herself would've been the first to say, on your – and, trust me, could she have spoken, her emphasis most certainly would have been on "your" – life. Yes, she spent more time on an orthopedic kitty bed on her favorite cellar shelf, eating specially prepared meals on one of those acrylic kitchen savers. But she would still hobble upstairs periodically to inspect the troops and rip out (no painstaking weeding for Tikvah) any insurrection. On one such expedition, Starfire, the young Siamese prima donna, came waltzing over to Tikvah with a big smirk on her elegant Sealpoint face. Clearly – Star is not a subtle feline, never has been, never will be – she was itching to show the old lady who was boss now.

The old lady gave Star a long hard "you-haven't-even-begun-to-earn-your-stripes-yet-Private" look. Star blanched – or would've if she could have – and backed off immediately. *Er – excuse me – I seem to remember I have some bugs to chase,* her expression said as she booked.

Tikvah sat there for some time after the Siamese had fled. She looked very pleased with herself. *Showed that foreigner, didn't I? Still got it.*

Did she ever. The story must've gone the rounds because none of the younger cats ever tried to mess with General Tikvah again. The insurrection stemmed, Tikvah seemed to enjoy her semi-retirement on the "apartment" shelf she sometimes shared with Kilah and Dervish. She was never as close them as she had been to Cricket, but they were old cronies now and had seen cats and kittens come and go. I could just imagine them reminiscing (*Say, do you remember when that mole got into the house, and we all went charging after it...?*) and playing kitty bingo, as Tom said.

Sometimes Tikvah would still head up to the second floor to soak up the sun in Marissa's bedroom. More often than not, though, I'd go down to the cellar and, stepping onto a chair, reach up and pat her. She was still, I assured her, my special girl. And while my fingers would be smoothing that pussywillow-colored fur of hers with its soft orange tinge, the same image kept coming to me: that of a limber, vibrant Tikvah making her way across a sunlit field.

Maybe – just maybe, I thought – it's a memory from the days before she came to live with us. But a long time afterwards, my friend Rita said, "Maybe she was trying to prepare you."

Maybe she was. A few months later, she went off her food all of a sudden. *If she doesn't start eating by tomorrow,* I told myself on the second night, *I'll take her in to see Tom.*

When the next morning came, I found her lying on her side on the cellar floor, still breathing but obviously in great pain. She looked up at me, and her eyes said it all: *I can't do this anymore.*

I dropped Marissa off at a friend's house and headed over to the clinic with Tikvah in the carrier on the seat next to me. Once there, I didn't hurry to take her in, just sat singing softly along to one of my favorite Bill Staines songs and talking to her. When the song was done, I simply played it again, touching her face gently through the carrier's grid door. We were outside of time, and I wanted to keep it that way....

Because once we were inside the examination room, time began moving all too quickly. "Renal lymphoma," Tom said, feeling her abdomen carefully. "There was no sign of it when she was in four months ago, but, then, it moves quickly in older cats."

There was no question in either of our minds as to what had to be done. The pain that had her in its grip now would be even more excruciating in a day or two. She'd had a long life with us, much longer than she would've had if she had not chosen to let go of her fear and find haven with us for eleven years.

"You want to stay?" Tom asked.

I nodded. Except in Jason's case, I had always stayed with my animals till the end, believing that I owed them that much. And in Tikvah's case, it mattered all the more. I did not want her to go out of this world feeling abandoned, as she'd been when I'd found her in the field.

Still, when the moment came and Tom was gently bringing the needle down for that last shot, I, who had been through this with so many other cats and dogs without crying, no matter how deeply the grief had cut, cried. Not great big gulping sobs, mind you, just little tears that spattered against my face like raindrops against a windowpane. Even for Cricket, my "best beloved" cat, I hadn't cried because tears, like love, just don't come easily to me. But for my old general-cat, my Tikvah-bus, I cried.

You taught me so much, I told her silently, tightening my hold on her. And just as the needle grazed her leg, she turned her head toward me, fastening her round green eyes on me with that peculiar fierce tenderness she'd shown precious few souls in her life. Even after the injection had done its work, those eyes did not close in a peaceful death-sleep, as I'd seen so many other animals' do. No, they remained open and fixed on me. I pressed my hands lovingly against her body and, incredibly, felt a deep purr vibrating through it.

I mentioned this to Tom. He shook his head. "No," he told me kindly, "she was gone at once." Sandy, my friend at Orphan Alley, a no-kill shelter out in Wisconsin, had another take on the subject, however. "You and Tikvah had such a close bond," she wrote back as soon as she'd received the news, "that it isn't surprising that you felt her communicate with you even after her heart stopped beating. Those bonds are forever."

Don't I know it. Sometimes, when I'm down in the cellar, I'll suddenly swivel around for no reason...no reason except that my heart expects to see a pair of ever-watchful pale-green owl eyes peering down at me from that old shadowy shelf of hers.

****

A few months after Tikvah hung up her double-pawed boxing gloves and went toward the light – I could just see her standing up on her hind legs, trying to gauge the distance – Cel and I were having a half-playful half-serious discussion about what she was up to in the hereafter. I said I thought she'd been given a post at the gates of Cat Heaven; there, she got to decide which felines got in and which ones had to go back and "try again." She did, of course, get to bop the latter back down to this earthly plane – which, knowing Tikvah as I did, I figured she must enjoy doing.

"It would be a sheer waste of administrative ability otherwise," Cel agreed.

Whatever she's up to in the Great Kitty Beyond, however, I know exactly what my old girl will do when I catch up with her, say, fifty or sixty years from now. She'll come running to me through a field of long tall celestial grasses shimmering green-gold in the sunlight. She'll stop just before she reaches me, sit down on her haunches, and look at me thoughtfully; then, slowly, she'll raise a front paw in greeting. And this time, in her owl eyes, I will see only joy and love, for the former things – the fear, the abuse, and the near-starvation – will have passed away.

THE HOUSE BLESSING

A lot of times, as I found out, you get a half-Abyssinian. Which is not a bad thing, mind you. But sometimes you get the whole Abyssinian.

I had wanted an Abyssinian cat ever since I'd read Gladys Taber's *Amber: A Very Personal Cat*. Granted, we did have Zorro, a charcoal-gray Aby-tabby mix who had wandered into our yard when he was 8-weeks-old and who, after checking our house out, had decided we were worth staying with. And despite his coloring and the conspicuous tabby stripes on his mottled coat, he had the agility, dexterity (he's the only one of our cats who has ever figured out that he needed to put his paw *around* a doorknob to make Things Happen), and highly intuitive way of communicating with people that, as I later learned, marked his purebred relations.

But my Abyssinian dream seemed destined to remain just that. After Tim's death, I went to a Cat Writers' Association (CWA) conference out in California and stopped in at the cat show next door. I found myself lingering by the Aby cages; later, I returned to the room I was sharing with fellow cat writer Sally Bahner and sheepishly took a handful of Aby breeder cards out of my pocket.

"I think it's a sign for you to get an Abyssinian cat," Sally remarked with amusement.

I chose to ignore the sign then. But the Abys found me anyhow. They're very determined that way. Watch them at a show sometime and notice how they keep trying to jimmy those locks on their cages. Three years later, I hooked up with a couple of Aby breeders, one of whom, Mary Ellen Hape, became a good friend and mentor. From her cattery, Singin', came Damiana, a Blue Aby kitten whom my cattery, Damiana-z, was named for, and Celtic Fire (a.k.a. Celtie), a Red Aby spay. And from another out-of-state cattery came an amber-eyed Ruddy kitten whom Marissa and I saddled with a name bigger than she was: Summer Solstice.

From the beginning, Solstice was an odd mixture of shyness and playfulness. She came across as being more self-effacing, less people-oriented than either Damiana or Celtie; but she was also the wise-guy kitten, the one who always started the wrestling matches and play-fights. She was under-sized and fighting an upper-respiratory infection that just wouldn't seem to quit. She'd go around the house making these snuffling snort-hog noises, which sounded bizarre coming from such a dainty feminine-looking kitten. Despite this, she managed to acquire an ardent beau in Topaz, our young Flamepoint Siamese. He was, and is, nuts about all our Aby girls – their little pointy faces and Dumbo ears apparently make his heart sing – but Solstice, with her scrappiness and her whiskers that were too big for her cougar face, was the Song of Songs, as far as he was concerned.

We lost beautiful big-eyed Damiana to some unforeseen genetic complications a few months before her first birthday. That left Solstice as the sole hope of out cattery. But she wasn't putting on weight, and my vet Tom had a hunch that those snort-hog noises might be due to a polyp in her throat, similar to one he'd removed from Damiana's. His hunch turned out to be uncannily on target: he removed a sizable polyp and pronounced Solstice ready to go to an upcoming cat show and then up to Mary's cattery in Rochester, New York for stud service.

What followed was probably the longest honeymoon in cattery history. Every week for three months, I called Mary for an update on Solstice's romance with a studly fawn male, only to learn that there wasn't any. Mary, who has a wicked sense of humor and a gift for turning a phrase that any writer might envy, summed it up like this: "She's there saying, 'Oh, no, I *can't* do that. I'm the Virgin Queen, and my mommy wouldn't let me.'"

Truth be told, Solstice sounded as forlorn as any child who'd been sent to summer camp or boarding school against her will: and my heart really did smite me every time Mary told me how pathetically eagerly my little "Cougar-ette" would greet her whenever she came into the room. And long-nosed Topaz wandered around the house, moping for his beloved.

But another, far more serious problem arose. Despite the surgery she'd gone through the previous March, Solstice was having trouble breathing again. A visit to Mary's vet confirmed that the polyp had come back in full force: in view of that fact, there seemed to be no point in putting her through the added stress of breeding. "Spay her," Mary told me over the phone. "Keep her as a pet and just love her."

No problem there. As I was driving up to the Sturbridge cat show a week later to pick Solstice up, I worried, though, that *she* wouldn't remember *us* after her three-month honeymoon-that-hadn't-been-a-honeymoon-at-all. But when I unlatched her carrier door, Solstice bolted straight out of it and up into my arms.

I knew you'd come, those eloquent amber eyes of hers said. *I knew you wouldn't forget me....*

"I never saw a cat so glad to be home," Mary said emphatically.

One hurdle jumped, two to go. First, there was the biopsy to make sure that the polyp wasn't malignant. *No,* I thought, remembering Damiana with her enormous far-seeing eyes and even more enormous ears, *not this one, too.* But the biopsy was negative, and Tom went ahead with the surgery, spaying her and removing a seven-ounce polyp. The wonder wasn't that she'd been going around making those ungodly noises but that she's been able to breathe at all.

She began vacuuming up food. Dry cat food, canned cat food, people food – it didn't matter. Solstice was an Aby with a mission, as far as eating went. *You never know,* the amber eyes would say as she quizzically sniffed a rice cake. By the time her stitches came out, her weight was up to 5.7 – a whole pound heftier than she'd been prior to this last operation.

I believe in signs. And Solstice's complete recovery, coming so soon after the loss of Damiana and several other family pets, was proof positive that we'd finally made our way out of that sad, dark grieving place. There *were* happy endings. Bad things *could* be turned around. And good things *did* happen to good kitties.

On my living room wall is a small gilt-framed piece of poetry entitled "The House Blessing." I never knew who wrote it, but the author certainly knew how to turn a phrase:

God bless the corners of this house,
And be the lintel blest;
And bless the hearth and bless the board
And bless each place of rest;
And bless the door that opens wide
To strangers as to kin;
And bless each crystal window pane
That lets the starlight in;
Ad bless the rooftree overhead
And every sturdy wall:
The peace of man, the peace of God,
The peace of love on all.

One morning – oh, maybe a month or two after the surgery – I happened to turn and see Solstice sitting on top of the radiator right under it. Always a pretty little cat, she had just then what I could only call a glow – a positive *aura* – that radiated from her big cougar-eyes straight down to her apricot underbelly.

"Are you 'The House Blessing'?" The words were out of my mouth before I realized it.

The amber eyes deepened appreciatively. *I was wondering when you'd notice*, they said gently.

Sometimes you get the whole Abyssinian. And sometimes, as in Solstice's case, you get a miracle.

CATSONG

Kilah looks my way as I come down the stairs in the morning. She hobbles out into the kitchen, ignoring the younger cats, and checks out the various food bowls. She eats more than usual: the appetite stimulant that my vet, Tom, gave her last week must be working. In between bites, she talks to me in that oddly Siamese-sounding voice of hers, something that she hasn't done all that often these last few months.

When I open the dishwasher, she hoists the upper part of her almost 17-year-old tortoiseshell body onto the door. It's a ritual she started years ago at the old house: after all, you never know when there's going to be margarine or something equally tasty still sticking to the utensils. After a quick look-see, Kilah eases herself back down onto the linoleum. She heads into the spare room, and I follow her, helping her into the litter box: her arthritis and the mass on her left hind leg make getting in there on her own a little tricky.

Later in the morning, I go back into the room to get started on some painting: I'm almost finished with the first coat on the window-frame when I realize I haven't heard that low *"Mer-row"* of hers for awhile. *She must be in the living room, soaking up the sun,* I think, then glance down. There's Kilah sitting next to my stepladder, looking up at me. *Did you think I'd go very far away?* her green eyes ask me gently.

It's a good day for my old lady. Last August, Tom removed a cancerous toe from that left hind foot. She came through surgery with her long striped tail waving high and renewed energy, exploring the upstairs in the new house for the first time. *So this is your bedroom. Nice,* the eyes said thoughtfully.

She began trailing me down to the cellar on my laundry runs. *Four litter boxes* — Kilah always had a very expressive face, due in part to her unusual yellow-and-white Phantom mask — *and a cat tree. Really. Carpeted down here, too. Much nicer than our old cellar.* Then she'd follow me back upstairs, one slow, careful step at a time, and go nap in the living room with Dervish and Zorro, the other old-timers.

Early this year, I noticed an abrasion on that same paw. Well, sometimes she did scratch herself. Her claws had a tendency to get too long: after all, she didn't move around a lot on account of her arthritis. But the area underneath the abrasion was puffed out and hairless. Tom wasn't too alarmed at first. But a blood test showed that the cancer was back.

Tom had taken care of our cats ever since Tim and I had brought Kilah and her sister, Cricket, in to him back in their barn-kitten days. That had been over 16 years ago. Since then, Tom had seen Marissa and me through personal tragedy and countless animal crises; and it was as both friend and vet that he discussed this new development with me. We were both against putting her through chemo. Nor did he feel that an amputation was an option. Kilah was too old to have to suddenly learn to get around on three legs.

"It's a slow-growing malignancy," he told me. "But surgery could cause it to grow faster." Kilah was a strong cat, he assured me: he wasn't ready to write her off yet.

Last Friday, I was carrying Kilah downstairs when my hand felt a mass in her left hind leg. Back to the clinic. The mass had actually been present at her last visit, Tom explained, and it hadn't changed. What worried him was that she'd lost a pound-and-a-half in a month's time, and, as he put it, she didn't have a lot of pounds-and-a-half left to lose. "It's going to happen," he said finally. "Today's not her day, though."

I have never had to help any of my cats "go gentle into that good night" like this. The others were all clearly in severe pain and going downhill rapidly when we made those last trips to the veterinary clinic. Kilah's decline has been slower, less obvious. It's difficult for me to gauge how much she's actually suffering.

And Kilah herself is trying so hard, forcing herself to get up, to greet us, to stay with us in body and in spirit as long as possible. *I won't leave you if you still need me*, the beautiful green eyes assure me. Her heart is still strong despite everything. So I will have to make the decision for both of us.

Almost 17 years....I can still see the wild little barn kitten who came to us with her equally wild little sister, the two of them wrestling with each other, sleeping on top of each other. Then I see Kilah as she is now, with that incredible love and serenity in her eyes, and a line from Edgar Lee Master's *Spoon River Anthology* – *"Some beautiful soul that lived life strongly"* – comes to me, and I think how well it suits her. *My old lady is going out in style,* I tell myself.

A week later, however, she's dragging herself from room to room with such obvious discomfort, I can't help wincing for her. Her hindquarters are pitifully gaunt, making her midsection seem barrel-like by contrast. She rallies later in the day: she eats almost a half-can of her favorite salmon cat food and lies purring by my side on the living-room sofa. Keisha, her adopted daughter, lies on top of me, stretched out in all her blue-tortie glory, touching her nose periodically to Kilah's whiskers in gentle concern. Marissa comes into the room and feels the old cat's body carefully, then leans her head close to her tortoiseshell side. "I think she should go in on Monday," my daughter says in that oddly adult way of hers.

A year ago, when Kilah's health problems started up, I was in a bad place. A lot of things had derailed on me, and I was still picking myself out of the wreckage. I rushed her to the vets' early one afternoon, thinking, *Not this, too. Don't die yet – give me one more year.*

There have been so many trips to the clinic with her since then. Each time, I've tried to mentally prepare myself for the possibility that this might be the end; each time, she has rallied, and it has been a not-so-minor miracle for me, a sign that things aren't always as bad as they seem.

The day after my talk with Marissa, Kilah rallies one last time. She has what I can only call "The Glow": her coat which has been so matted and hard to keep up, is suddenly kitten-silky under my fingertips again. She's walking much better, and even the abraded nodule on that hind foot seems to have miraculously healed over. A chill runs through me as I look at her, knowing what I'm seeing is a feline version of that inexplicable incandescence that terminally ill people have at the end of their journeys. It fades away within the hour, and we continue our death-watch.

Monday finally comes. Marissa goes to school, and I have my own private good-bye with Kilah before we drive over to the clinic. Stroking her, I realize that it has indeed been about a year since the day I begged her not to die. "Thank you for keeping your promise and staying that extra year," I tell her simply. "I'll stay with you till the end."

And I do. I wrap my arms around her as she lies on the table and lean in as close to her as I possibly can. Her purr vibrates through her anemic fluid-filled body long after she has left it, leaving me with one last song.

"The end of an era," Tom sighs. He looks down at her. "A beautiful cat...a beautiful spirit."

It's a good epithet.

****

Late one night, maybe two weeks after Kilah's death, I'm having trouble sleeping. I'm just about to settle back down when I hear a low, deep "*MER-ROW.*"

Only one of our cats has ever had a miaow like that. Tim and I used to laugh about it. It was a Lauren Bacall miaow, always sounding like a very insistent "ME NOW!"

But of course, what I'm hearing now can't be Kilah.

It comes a second, then a third time. One of the cats must be stuck somewhere, I think. Sighing, I swing my legs out of bed, and the rest of me tiredly follows.

I check each room. All of the other cats are fast asleep. There is no logical answer for the miaow.

I've heard it a few times since that night. And I'm aware of a presence – a very gentle, familiar one – that follows me about the house. I know, without knowing how I know, that Kilah has not left us yet. I kept my promise about staying with her till the end: she's still keeping hers.

OLD FRIENDS

Dervish hops up next to me on the breezeway sofa. He purrs companionably while I have my morning coffee, then rests his large orange-and-white head on my wrist till it's time for me to get to work. He's 14 pounds now – a far cry from his 22-pound Great Pumpkin magnificence in his prime – and sometimes his thick coat gets matted and needs comb intervention. But those things don't matter between old friends. And we do go back a long time, Derv and I: it has been 16 years since he came to us as a round-eyed rambunctious kitten that his former owner was anxious to unload.

Later in the morning, I go upstairs to check on Zorro, who's sleeping in Marissa's room. The heat has been troubling him, and his appetite is a bit off. He peers up at me, purrs, and goes back to sleep. He, too, has lost weight and tone with age, and his sight is blurred from cataracts. We go back a long ways, too, Zorro and I: it has been 15 years since he wandered out of the woods by our old house, a fearless, friendly kitten-adventurer.

Derv and Zorro, along with Woody (a mere 12-years-old and a former stray himself), are the last of the Old Guard. The rest of our feline familiars – a motley gang of Abyssinians, Siamese, and good ol' garden-variety moggies – are considerably younger. Oh, they're loving, exasperating personalities in their own right, with more idiosyncrasies than a whole slew of Dickens characters; and someday, they, too, will be the Old Guard. But Derv and Zorro were there almost from the beginning, even before Marissa was born....

Derv came to us when Tim and I had been married about two years. Actually, I snuck him into the house while Tim was taking part in a training program out in Milwaukee: at the time, we had just the two barn-cat sisters, Cricket and Kilah, and he was adamant about keeping it that way. So were the sisters, who'd gotten all bottle-brush-tailed about other cats we'd briefly taken care of for friends. And, in theory, I agreed with them.

But I forgot all about theory when I saw the ad for a deaf kitten in need of a home. I could just picture him, all drooping whiskers and forlorn face like the sad-eyed kitten pictures of my childhood. Before I knew it, I was reaching for the phone.

The kitten who showed up in our kitchen that afternoon was white with a red-tabby mask and patches. He was so young, his eyes were still blue. He wasn't in the least pathetic – he began shadow-boxing with his reflection in the dishwasher door almost immediately – and there definitely wasn't anything wrong with his hearing.

What he was absolutely adorable. Even Tim conceded as much when he came home from Milwaukee... right before he told me that the newcomer had to go. He even lined up a potential taker: his sister, Carolyn, who lived in New Hampshire.

Carolyn came down, took a look at the orange-and-white fur ball half-asleep in the laundry basket, asked him what he thought of the name "MacGyver" – then suddenly concluded it was too hot that particular day to subject him to the long trip north. By then, Dervish (Tim had given him the name on account of his antics, especially his crimes against toilet paper) had been with us a few weeks: I think Carolyn, who misses very little, saw that he already had us in his over-sized paws, and no more was ever said about a name change and transfer.

But we still had a sizable problem to deal with. Derv, for all his calendar-kitten cuteness, was "wild for to hold" and clearly had tiger fantasies. Translated, he was a biter. *That*, and not his supposed deafness, we realized, had been why his first owner had been so eager to send him on his way. One night, shortly after Carolyn's visit, Tim was lying on the sofa in his robe, telling me a story, when he suddenly yelped with pain. Within seconds, Derv scurried around the sofa and out into the kitchen, looking incredibly pleased with himself: he had snuck under Tim's robe and bit him on the butt. A real *coup* for a kitten.

Gradually, we were able to tame him down. He was still extremely playful, though; and the "Ladies of the Club" – Cricket, Kilah, and Tikvah, a 1 ½-year-old stray who'd recently joined their ranks – weren't. Then Zorro wandered into our yard and decided that any yard with a catnip bed that close to the bird feeder (a definite miscalculation on my part) had real potential.

The wayfaring kitten was roughly eight-weeks-old and had suspiciously Abyssinian-looking ears, eyes, and mottling to go along with the charcoal-colored tabby stripes on his face, chest and legs. I brought him into the kitchen and gave him some food and water; then, mindful that it hadn't been all that long since I'd gotten Tikvah clearance, put him back outside. But the kitten had Ideas, and they did not include leaving. He kept returning to the back-porch steps and working his expressive green eyes. *You seem like such a nice human....*

He worked his charms even harder when Tim came home from work. My husband had just given him a temporary visa when the phone rang: Tim sat down on the loveseat to take the call, which happened to be a work-related one, and Zorro, wide-eyed opportunist that he was, curled up confidingly on Tim's right shoulder and fell asleep. Tim was a cat person, and that melted him in nanoseconds. Zorro wasn't going anywhere.

Derv was delighted. He would lie in wait under a chair or the bed, stretch out a long white paw, and grab his new little buddy. A glorious wrestling match would follow. Derv also displayed a curiously paternal attitude toward Zorro and would groom him as fastidiously as a mother cat before setting to work on his own fur. They'd spend hours together, napping companionably together or stretched out on the wide windowsills of the enclosed back porch...no doubt discussing Zorro's Adventures Out in the Wild, Tikvah's bossiness, or Derv's brief romance with Silver Bear, a beautiful stray who *had* gone to live with Carolyn, only to give birth to five kittens shortly afterward. (Carolyn always suspected Derv of having been the father – he'd met Silver Bear shortly before he was neutered – and threatened him with a paternity suit; I countered by saying that we'd have to haul Ms. Bear in for corrupting a minor.)

Derv was the extrovert, the official greeter, and all-around huggable guy. He loved everybody, and everybody loved him. Once, I actually woke up to find him sleeping in between Tim and myself, his grapefruit-sized head all nice and comfy on the pillow. And, as he grew into what my mother-in-law, Bobbie, called "a Portly Paws," he truly didn't mind if you used *him* as a pillow... provided that you rested just the side of your face ever-so-gently against his well-padded flank. Later, when Marissa appeared on the scene, Derv would lie in her Pack 'n' Play and let her put her tiny feet up on him.

Zorro, on the other hand, went from being a friendly, talky kitten – he used to make these funny little "*Nyeh-nyeh-nyeh*" speeches to apprise us of his and Mr. Lion's (a small toy animal that he was fond of dragging about the house) whereabouts – to being something of a brooding loner. Even though he wasn't a purebred, he developed a more than purebred attitude. Incredibly striking with his subtle mix of Abyssinian and tabby markings, he was "bad but beautiful," Bobbie declared. (He'd clawed her stockings at their first meeting.) He became very territorial, spraying anything that he felt needed reclaiming. Usually, that meant Tim's stuff, which obviously put a big strain on their relationship. Tim frequently rued the day he'd fallen for the deceptively sweet-looking kitten asleep on his shoulder. "We could always sell him as a rare Black Abyssinian," my husband would reflect aloud, a speculative look in his blue-green eyes.

Yet for all his bad but beautiful ways, Zorro had a great gift: he was a paws-on healer. After I'd had a bad day, he would seemingly materialize out of nowhere and lie on my chest: the tension would ebb out of me almost immediately. At first, I wrote it off as my imagination; now that I've studied Reiki, I don't. Some people possess a healing touch – "golden hands," as my grandmother used to say – so why not Zorro? Cats are so alive to warmth, to the vibrations of worlds seen and unseen, they're the perfect energy conductors.

Changes came to us. Woody and Boris, two other strays, joined us. We had Marissa. Then, when she was 3 ½, Tim was killed in a car accident, and all was, to paraphrase Yeats, changed, changed utterly. Eventually, we packed up our memories and animals and left the old house. By this time, several of our old-timers – Cricket, Tikvah, and Boris – had left us for celestial catnip beds (hopefully, from their perspective, with bird-feeders right next to them) – and others had come to ease the loneliness their going had left behind. And front and center were Kilah, Derv, and Zorro, who'd been with us since the beginning.

We lost Kilah to cancer two years after the move. But Derv and Zorro are still here, living, loving connections to that other time. They're thinner than they were, and they make a lot more trips to see Tom than they used to. Derv needs to be dosed nightly for his mega-colon condition. He is also considerably less patient with the younger cats, frequently retreating to his private lair (an old bureau/cabinet with one lower door missing and a fleecy orthopedic blanket inside) when their rowdiness gets on his nerves. Zorro spends part of each winter on Clavamox for his chronic upper-respiratory infections and no longer gets scolded for occasional spraying: his failing eyesight has given him a built-in alibi.

But Derv still fills the house with his presence: he inspects everything that's going on, purring loudly. And snoring even more loudly: I can still hear him several rooms away. Zorro, who has mellowed back into being the affectionate character that wandered out of the woods that summer day, continues to do his paws-on healing.

Sometimes I've put off writing about certain cats: then, suddenly, they're gone, leaving only memory where there were once warm, purring presences. Anne in Margaret Campbell Barnes's *My Lady of Cleves* (a delightful but out-of-print novel, well worth looking up) reflects "that when people are parting it is best to speak straight from the heart lest one should withhold some ultimate tenderness until it be too late." Hopefully, it'll be a long while before Derv, Zorro, and I come to that seemingly final parting that's so hard to see beyond.

But old friends – endearing quirks, faulty lines, and all – still need to be celebrated. Sluggish colons, cataracts, chronic sinus problems (mine as well as Zorro's!), C-sections scars, and life lessons, we are all the worse – or better – for wear. And that, as the Velveteen Rabbit learned, is when things become Real.

HEART & SOUL

When Cricket died, I felt as if she'd taken her share of my heart with her. She'd been with me through marriage, motherhood, widowhood, and the launching of my career as a writer, and now, suddenly, she was gone. No loving cat presence hanging out at the computer with me or tripping the kitty fantastic down the stairs alongside me, waiting for me to pull up a step with her and scratch the plushy brownish-gray tiger fur she was so justifiably vain about. No understanding amber eyes or crackling purr to help me through the blue moods, the endless gray days. She had been my solace, my heart's ease, and, above all else, my Soul. And now that Soul had departed from my house, leaving it empty and echoing.

But there was still Tikvah – demanding, fearful, loyal double-pawed Tikvah, who looked enough like Cricket to have been her litter-mate. She eased the pain following Cricket's death with her own funny, fierce devotion. I could never pick her up without her growing six extra paws and flailing about, a sign of the abuse she must've received in a previous life. But I could hold her in such a way that she came to understand that I wouldn't hurt her, and she followed me about like a four-footed shadow, carrying on a pretty constant stream of conversation.

She taught me in her own way about love and its shadow side, fear...how sometimes you had to take hold of that fear to get to the love.

Three years later, Tikvah was gone, too. Oh, we had other cats -- each one a quirky, colorful personality in his or her own right – but no one who was my special crony, as Cricket and Tikvah had been. Then Solstice stepped to the forefront.

Actually, she'd been doing her own little paw-shuffle toward me even before Tikvah had died. The Ruddy Abyssinian had been a sickly kitten – due, as it turned out, to a polyp in her throat that my vet, Tom, removed – so I'd been feeding her by hand and fussing over her in general. It had built a bond between us, although I didn't realize how strong that bond was till she went up to my friend Mary's cattery in Rochester for an enforced honeymoon and ended up staying for three months. I missed her terribly; Solstice was homesick and not, she made it clear to her intended, that big on arranged marriages. She came home with her virginity intact and another, even bigger polyp in her throat.

She also came back knowing that in her delicate little Abyssinian bones that she was my cat. When I opened the carrier that day, wondering if she'd even remember us, she bolted up out of the carrier into my lap, the love leaping out of her huge eyes...eyes that were as amber and glowing as my Cricket's had been.

Her next operation was a complete success: this time, Tom was able to remove the entire polyp, and Solstice finally started gaining some desperately needed weight. Then she began to pick up where Cricket had left off, even adopting my old girl's habits of coming down the stairs with me a few steps at a time and helping with the weekly bed-changing...helping, meaning in her case, as it had in Cricket's, tunneling under the fresh sheets or leaping on them, ready for the imaginary kill, the moment I tried to straighten them out. She had the same thoughtful understanding in her glance and her manner. It was as if my tigery old barn cat and this aristocratic little showgirl had somehow melded into one. I started calling her "Sol" for short, not even thinking about the pun or the truth therein.

But, over time, it has come to me: she *is* my soul, my kindred spirit in a fur suit, the one who will rush to my side when the world is askew and I have, in the words of the old song, "wounds to bind". She is my familiar in the best sense of the word, just as Cricket was.

Dawn came to us from Mary's cattery nine months after Solstice's last operation, just as winter was giving way to spring. I'd once joked that I wanted to some day adopt a black female cat and name her "D. B. Dawn" – Darkest Before the Dawn" – but there was nothing dark about this Dawn. She was an incredibly petite Red Abyssinian female with just a touch of gold to her coat and golden eyes that seemed almost too big for her pointy little face. She was, as Solstice had been, skittish at first but quickly came around, burrowing under the bedcovers and getting up close and personal with me when she felt like having a bit of company at night.

After her first heat, she returned to Mary's for breeding and stayed up there almost as long as Solstice had. But Dawn came back pregnant and, just a couple of days before Valentine's Day, gave birth to a single Ruddy Aby kitten, Aspen, whose legs just looked way too short for her furry butterball body. Marissa and I used to joke that pretty soon, Ms. Aspen would be so big, *she*'d be carrying her tiny mama around by the nape of *her* neck.

Aspen was an enchantment, no way around it. We willingly gave up hours every evening to kitten-watching, delighted when she opened her eyes and began to recognize us...cracking up when she and Dawn had these endless squeak-and-squeal conversations in "the nursery" (a.k.a. the spare room) or when she managed to squeeze her pudginess through the sizeable gap under the door and escape into the hallway.

So, when she died so suddenly one March night – probably from a viral infection or a congenital defect, Tom said, although I chose not to have an autopsy done – she broke our hearts, and we mourned as though we'd lost a human baby. Dawn wandered through the house, making plaintive little cries that cut through us with stiletto sharpness. As heart-wrenching as those cries were, however, even worse were the times when she paced through the empty nursery, not making a sound, her golden eyes puzzled and forlorn.

"She's trying to make sense of why all that happened," animal healer Gigi Kast explained shortly afterwards. "Even though the spiritual self was acquiescent, she has to deal with it on an emotional and physical level." Like us, she was learning a hard lesson in resiliency and in trusting the process.

Gradually, Dawn began to put on a little weight, to play with her toys again, and to run races with the other young cats. Her golden-red fur regained its gloss, and her eyes started to lose their brooding, searching look. Little more than a kitten herself, she was learning to be happy again. And she was all the more loving for what she had gone through.

Not long ago, Marissa came home from a tag sale with a little gray-and-white kitten whom she promptly dubbed Gremlin. Dawn gave a perfunctory hiss, then sat back, her large gold eyes rapt. Spell-bound. You could almost see her mulling it all over, weighing the possibilities that this anything-but-Abyssinian-looking kitten suggested. By evening, she had adopted him and was happily washing him. And Gremlin? He was trotting around adoringly after his new mom and squealing delightedly during their wrestling matches.

About a week later, Katherine, the little girl whom we'd gotten him from, came over to see how he was doing. I knew that her family was moving soon: and out of curiosity, I asked if they were taking the mother cat with them.

Katherine shook her head. "She ran away eight weeks ago. We can't find her."

So the kitten who had brought that glow back to Dawn's eyes had needed her as much as she had needed him. Each had filled the other's emptiness—each had given the other something to love.

If Solstice is my brand-new Soul, then Dawn is—not my Shadow, as Tikvah was -- but my Heart. We've both experienced motherhood, love, and loss, and struggled our way through that last one. When she comes to me now and walks over my work, demanding a head-scritch or snuggles under the blankets next to me, purring, I can't help smiling to myself, no matter what kind of day it has been. She is not the Darkest-Before-the-Dawn cat that I once joked about, although she knows a lot about that particular brand of darkness. No, she is my Dawntreader, my Dawnstar who has taught me about taking heart...about that heart's being broken wide-open and hope, faith and joy taking root in it. Especially joy.

DAWNSTAR

Slipping through the afternoon
shadows, quick-pawed
& lithe,
my Dawn-cat
leaps up on the bed
next to me.
Red-gold but more gold than red,
she rubs her tiny Abyssinian face
against mine,
chasing away the
cobwebs in the attic of my mind .
Kittenless now,
she senses grief&joy
&, like the sweetest chord
on a dulcimer,
she burbles blessing
into the stillness
of the room.
She is my golden girl,
my flirty furry muse,
my yellow-eyed North Star
guiding me through
the rainy days,
the storms of heart&soul.

STORM'S PASSING

For Stormy (2000-2004), whose heart stopped
unexpectedly one June morning.

After a storm's passing,
the air is calm,
almost considerate,
the colors sharper,
& the shore peaceful
beyond reckoning.
But when you
with your Ruddy Abyssinian
face, quizzical green eyes,
& playful, bounding spirit
passed out of our lives
so suddenly,
so inexplicably,
you left a grief
too big for us to hold.
Your afterglow
lingers, shimmering
in the swishing field grasses
that you, an indoor cat,
could not explore;
in the yellowred&orange daylilies,
almost as vibrant as you;
in all places wild
& untamable.
You, with your cougar grace
& satiny coat,
left us bereft
on a lonely shore,
our world all the grayer
for your going.

WOODRUFF X. STRAY

For Tim

Woody lies next to me on the sofa, covering half of my writing portfolio with his black-spotted white body. *Going to write, were you?* his yellow eyes inquire. *I don't think so.* He has, he indicates gently, no plans of budging. *You may, however, pet me.*

That's Woody for you – low-keyed but persistent. He has a voice, all right, but he tends to save it for things that matter...such as sweet-talking susceptible humans into giving a down-on-his-luck young cat a home.

He was roughly 8-months-old when he wandered into Tim's vegetable garden and good graces over 13 years ago – definitely feral but friendly, too, and more than willing to pass the time with a sociable human. He started visiting Tim on a regular basis. I was aware of him: we had a slew of strays coming into our yard that year, but Woody stood out by virtue of those huge spots on his dazzling white fur. He acknowledged me – I was, after all, the bringer of food – but he zeroed in on Tim. Smart move, seeing as my husband was the one he'd have to get clearance from.

We had five cats then, and Tim was pretty adamant about there being no more room at the inn. So I kept quiet, put food out for the strays, and worried about them when the weather was bad.

"You know, that is a nice cat," Tim observed one day after a visit from his black-and-white buddy. "Really friendly."

"Oh," I said.

"Wonder if he belongs to anyone," Tim said casually maybe a week later. He paused. "Maybe we should kidnap him." Within days of that conversation, Woody was installed as a permanent resident. An outdoorsy name seemed called for, so I named him "Woodruff" after the white-flowered herb in my garden; and Tim, who loved punning, added the "X. Stray."

Woodruff X. Stray liked me. He liked Marissa...though there was probably a slightly ulterior motive mixed in with his liking, especially as she moved on to solid foods. When she graduated to chopped-up hotdogs, the former stray positioned himself faithfully by her highchair and waited for the manna to land: *This is great. Wait till the old gang outside hears about this.* Then, after days and days of hotdog fall-out, Woody finally walked away. *I will eat no more hotdogs forever,* the dismissive swish of his plumy black tail said.

Not that that interfered with his liking of Marissa. He was, as I've said, a very sociable guy and liked to greet everybody. Once, my mother-in-law was babysitting Marissa. Marissa was napping, so Bobbie – who believed, she always said, in "letting sleeping babies lie" – made herself comfortable in the gooseneck rocker with a magazine. Suddenly, out of nowhere came Woody. He jumped up on her lap, then, realizing they hadn't Been Properly Introduced, licked her right on the lips and high-tailed it down. *Mustn't overdo this interspecies thing.*

But he was, first and foremost, Tim's cat. Tim had taken him in. Tim was the one he followed about. Of course, Tim was also the one he stole food from on a regular basis. A good-natured con, Woody was never one to let affection interfere with business. One evening, Tim dallied out in the yard, talking to neighbors instead of coming right in for dinner. Tired of waiting – when Tim was telling a story, God couldn't have shut him up -- I left his chicken pie on the table and went upstairs to put Marissa to bed. "How was the pie?" I asked absently over my book when he came up much later.

"The *crust*" – Tim mustered up all the sarcasm he could, which was considerable – "was fine."

"The crust?" I looked up blankly.

"I thought you'd taken the filling out because I was late for dinner," he explained sheepishly.

I shook my head. "I might've yelled at you," I said, "but I wouldn't have *starved* you."

The real culprit was soon discovered and not too far away from the crime scene. Woody had Hoovered every last smidgen of chicken-pie filling out, leaving just the crust. Crust was fattening, he assured us, as he finished polishing off his paws.

He took to sitting on the table, right next to Tim's plate. In fact, he was such a regular, Tim began to comment on his absences. "Woody's not here," my husband would say, staring suspiciously at his meal. "I'm not eating."

Woody's thievery and klutziness -- whenever the "cow cat" jumped up on the bookcase or a bureau, he inevitably took down a few ornaments and pictures with that long plumy tail of his – aside, Tim loved him. "Just looking at him," he'd say, "makes me smile."

Then Tim died, and Woody the loving and lovable withdrew into himself. I was so overwhelmed by the tragedy and by having to suddenly raise Marissa by myself, I didn't notice it right away. When I did, I saw eyes as full of sadness as any human's, and I tried to make up for all the time he'd been left to grieve by himself.

Gradually, he transferred his affection to me. Then Star, an uppity 10-week-old Sealpoint Siamese, came into his life. Star, who was missing Mom and the littermates, took one look at Woody and latched right on to him. And I do mean "latched": I'd wake up to weird noises in the night and find her at the foot of my bed, nursing on him. I'm still not sure why Woody let her do it. Perhaps it had to do with the fact that he was still feeling very vulnerable. Or maybe Star didn't listen to his objections and just went ahead and did what she wanted. She's like that.

Whatever the reason, they soon became an item. And an item they have remained to this day, Star snuggling up against Woody one moment and cuffing him without warning the next. It's a challenging relationship, further complicated by the fact that Woody now has the biggest crush on our littlest cat, Dawn. He is caught between a Siamese and an Abyssinian, and, as he tells us in plaintive miaows, that is Infinitely Harder than being caught between an Old Rock and a Hard Place – especially when That Siamese is Star.

But, on the whole, he is happy, he tells me now in a series of burbling purrs. (There's a goodly sprinkling of white hairs on his black ears – courtesy of Star, we assume – but I don't mention those.) The phone rings, so I have to get up, upsetting both Woody and the notebook. I come back a little later and get back on the sofa, ready to return to my rough draft. Before I can pull the notebook over to me, however, Woody is on it. Literally. He is now covering the *whole* portfolio, not just half of it. He glances up at me, his yellow eyes shining. Tim was right: just looking at him makes me smile.

SOUL-CAT

She talks to me with her eyes – those incredibly sweet almond-shaped amber eyes. It's an Aby trick: even Zorro, our half-Abyssinian cat, does it. And Solstice, my Ruddy girl, has never used her voice much until now.

She scarfs down some chicken, then wanders down cellar. A little later, when Marissa and I are sitting at the picnic table in the backyard, I glance up to see Solstice sitting in the kitchen window. *Just wanted to know where you were,* her eyes say as they shift from honey amber to moss amber and back again to honey.

My beloved Soul-Cat is dying. She is only five-years-old; but she's in kidney failure, the bane of so many Abyssinians. I don't know exactly how much longer we have together, only that every moment is achingly precious.

Until a few weeks ago, we had no idea that she was in danger. We were treating her for a badly abscessed tooth, and she seemed to be responding to the antibiotics. One day, I found a cat fang lying on Marissa's bureau and figured that that was the end of Solstice's tooth problem.

Then I noticed that she'd lost her cougar sleekness. Her beautiful Ruddy coat with its apricot underbelly suddenly felt as loose and woolly as the jacket an old beau had given me. Nice in the jacket but somehow not quite right in the Aby.

That's when a trip to the emergency vet clinic revealed the underlying problem: kidney failure. Both my heart and mind fought the news. Solstice had been my little miracle cat: I had hand-fed her as a sickly kitten and seen her through two surgeries for throat polyps when she'd been just a year old. She, in turn, had made it clear that she was a one-person cat and that I was that person, following me around and performing kitty Reiki or push-paws on me when I was resting....

This time, I know, there will be no miracle for my Solstice. But we do not have to say good-bye just yet.

The other cats seem to understand that Solstice is ill but take the matter in their furry stride. They sit with her on the kitchen counter, watching the birds at the feeders together, or sun themselves with her in the breezeway.

Marissa and I have gotten the hydrating-and-medicating process down pretty well now. I'm feeding Solstice baby food – sometimes from a spoon, sometimes from my fingers – and Nutri-Cal. Her coat has regained some of its gloss, although it still has a rumpled dandruff-y look. Tom sees an improvement in her attitude, if not in her kidney values: at her last visit, she kicked over our over-stuffed file folder and looked smug as the tech was picking the papers up. *See what happens when you mess with me? Don't you ever think about sticking me with that thermometer again....* She is, as Tom says, "a scrappy cat despite her condition.... I wouldn't give up hope."

Still, there's a certain amount of letting go I have to do. Little rituals...such as our going up and downstairs together a few steps at a time or my giving her the corn silk and shucks to play with when we're having fresh corn...that we have to put aside now that her energy level is so much lower. No more Solstice playing cave kitty in the sheets while I'm changing the bed or doing her kitty Reiki. No more glancing down when I wake up in the middle of the night to see her sleeping in the cubbyhole of my night table.

Now I do Reiki on her when she's up for it and letting her rest when she's not. But, on her good days, Solstice sits there, her almond-shaped eyes glowing. I assure her that she is still beautiful. That she has my heart.

Her eyes deepen. *Of course,* they say. *You gave it to me a long time ago. No take-backs.*

No take-backs. For all the pain of letting her go, I wouldn't have it any other way. Love is, as the Song of Songs says, strong as death. Stronger. And therein lies the miracle.

It's easy to lose sight of that miracle in the days that follow, however. Solstice has begun to fight our hydrating her, throwing up immediately afterward. And the process itself seems to be doing her less and less good: her body's sucking up the fluid almost as soon as it goes in.

One night, just before I head upstairs, I go over to Solstice, who's resting on the kitchen counter. Gently, I pat her. She turns toward me and begins rubbing her face against my hand. She keeps doing this till there's a kind of rhythm to it. *Love you, too,* the big amber eyes say. *My human.* When I move over to the other side of the counter, she makes herself get up and follow me. Then she begins nuzzling my hand all over again. It's as if she can't stop. Won't stop.

The next day, she's so congested, she can't even smell her baby food. Depressed, I go out to run errands, anything to escape the pain threatening to overtake me. Ten minutes down the road, I hear a voice say, "Go back." And, like Solstice the night before, it doesn't let up.

Finally, I turn around and go home. I give Solstice her antibiotic early, figuring that that might just break the congestion up enough for her to eat. It works. She manages to get some shredded chicken down, then rubs her head against my hand. *Thank you. You came back for me. You always do.*

My heart still does this horrible lurch inside me when I look at her and see a little ghost-cat where not so very long ago, there was a beautiful Ruddy cougar of an Aby. But I'm suddenly glad that I listened to that voice – that I went back and faced the pain instead of running from it.

When I bring her in to see Tom the next morning, her mouth has become necrotic. She's anemic, and there's a strong uremic odor permeating her coat. Once a sleek 9 ½ pounds, she now weighs about as much as a six-month-old kitten.

Tom can't find a vein on her, so he gives her a slow-working abdominal injection. Then we wrap Solstice gently in a towel. "I'm so sorry," I tell her, my eyes and voice clogged with tears.

"You did everything you could," Tom says. He sighs. "I really thought she had a chance. She put up a good fight." He leaves the room so that I can have the time remaining – maybe 10 minutes or so – alone to hold and talk to her.

Solstice squirms at first. Affectionate as she is, she doesn't care much for being held. Finally, she settles down in my arms. I talk to her, even pray a little.

Slowly, Solstice puts her head down on my breast and keeps it there. I never know the exact instant that she dies, only that the room is suddenly awash with peace and love. That by holding her till the end and then some – by going with her as far on her journey as I can – death has somehow changed its shape and is no longer a cruel, fearsome bogey to shrink from. This is just one more gift that she has given me.

****

But not the last. About a week later, I'm out in my backyard, raking. Suddenly, I see Solstice. Every detail is as finely limned as in a painting. She's sitting at the edge of my meditation garden, beautiful and glowing in her autumnal colors. I can even see the silky apricot underbelly that she loved having stroked. Her tail is wrapped around her paws, and she simply radiates love and happiness. I can almost hear her burble.

The image keeps coming in stronger and stronger. And for the first time since I learned that she was dying, I feel happy. Or, rather, I can *feel* her happiness as though it was my own. It's as though she's inside me and not just figuratively: a physical warmth suffuses me.

She keeps appearing to me in the weeks that follow. I'll be out driving – or raking – or walking – and, suddenly, she's there. In ghostly tales, you know a spirit is present because of the eerie chill that cuts thorough you. But with Solstice, there is only that incredible inrush of warmth....

A long time ago, I christened Solstice my "House Blessing" because her complete recovery from her throat polyps marked the end of a sad, dark time when we'd lost several beloved family pets. And, truly, ever since our souls touched and melded over five years ago, everything about Solstice has been a blessing to me. Even now, it seems, my little cat has a miracle or two up her paw.

All at once, I get it. The miraculous is always around us: it's just that the nature of the miracles changes. Many of them are as quiet and understated as a loving amber-eyed Abyssinian who used to wait for me to come in from my morning run. We only know they're miracles because of that feeling of "unexpected grace" that they inevitably bring with them...the way they stop time and reveal the soul of things.

My House Blessing is still with me, as magical and flame-bright as ever. The body is gone, but the spirit is more than willing.

FOR SOLSTICE

(April 15, 1999 -- September 9, 2004)

You come to me
in the garden
skimming silently
across the falling leaves.
I turn,
& there you are,
every Abyssinian inch of you
from glowing amber eyes
to silky apricot belly
finely limned as in a
painting.
Your dark-tipped whip of a tail
wrapped about your ghost-paws,
you sit there,
quiet & loving-eyed
as in life,
& our souls touch once again
in greeting.
All roads do not
end in death, you tell me:
soul-knots cannot be untied.
Your cougar-lithe body
 is gone,
but your spirit lingers,
as magical -- & as real --
as roses in November.

LEAPS OF FAITH

He is not show quality. His hind feet are over-sized, clearly designed for a larger cat. He is a toilet paper-shredder and wallpaper border- and wire-chewer. (He took down Marissa's mini-stereo, and the electrified houses in our miniature Halloween village gave up their low-wattage ghosts and spooky lights shortly after his arrival.) He is not graceful and has more failed counter jumps than not to his credit. As for bathtubs..."When *hasn't* he fallen in?" my 14-year-old observes sarcastically.

Which has in no way stopped Phoenix from trying. He is a great believer in leaps of faith. O. K., so he frequently slam-dunks himself into the kitchen floor. But sometimes – especially when it counts, like at feeding time – he does conquer the counter. Clearly, he doesn't care to dwell on the misses. Onward and upwards is his motto – even if he does end up downwards and splay-pawed a few times first.

Phoenix came to us following my beloved Solstice's death. Shortly after Tom confirmed that Solstice's kidneys were failing and rapidly, I contacted Mary at Aby Central (known to the outside world as Singin' Cattery) in Rochester, New York. Once Solstice was gone, we would be without a Ruddy Abyssinian, and I couldn't bear the thought. I love the Aby in all its colors, but something about the Ruddys with their cougar grace and warm autumnal coloring had always especially appealed to me. Did Mary have any pet-quality Ruddys?

Mary did. A year-old already neutered male who, she said, needed more love than she could give him, given the demands of the cattery. She would keep him for us until our vigil with Solstice was over.

The end of that vigil came much sooner than we had expected. About a month later, we found ourselves driving back from Boxboro, Massachusetts with one highly indignant Aby male. He wasn't loud like a Siamese, of course -- I don't think that the Abys can hit those piercing Yoko Ono notes that their Siamese brethren can – but he was pretty insistent, nonetheless. Since I was concentrating on the highway, I missed the gist of his plaintive commentary, but I'm pretty sure he said something about contacting Interpol.

Still, Phoenix seemed to settle in reasonably well once we got home. He happily bopped along with the Younger Gang -- Gremlin, Rory, and Hawkeye. In fact, he soon decided that Hawkeye, who was about the same age, was His Long-Lost Littermate. The fact that Hawkeye with his silver-streaked black fur wouldn't have passed for an Aby in any universe didn't trouble Phoenix in the least. They had, Phoenix informed his new bro, Been Separated at Birth, probably by – this was said with a quick glance at Star, whom Phoenix had enough sense to be wary of –an Evil Siamese.

No foolin,' said Hawkeye, who was very impressed by this upgrade in his pedigree.

It's true, Phoenix assured him and proceeded to paw-wrestle him to the floor. After all, what else were brothers for?

On the whole, I figured we were in for a relatively peaceful transition. So I was shocked when Phoenix developed a food allergy and scratched so much, he began looking more like a moth-eaten teddy bear than a miniature cougar. I changed the cats' diet, working in some lamb baby food because, according to Tom, that was about as hypoallergenic as you could get. I dabbed Phoenix with every salve and ointment imaginable; when those didn't work, I took him in to the veterinary clinic for steroid shots.

It felt like a never-ending battle, coming as it did so soon after Solstice's last illness. And – it sounded silly, but there it was – he wasn't Solstice. I found myself missing her more than ever. Solstice, for all her shyness, had been deeply loving, shadowing me up and down the stairs and sharing all sorts of silly, playful rituals with me. You know – the kind you have when you've been together a long time and know each other inside-out. Phoenix was friendly enough but came across as being more of a cat's cat and not all that interested in people.

Which only goes to show how wrong I was. The little guy with the big feet was actually having more trouble getting adjusted to his new environment than I realized. And he was trying, in the only way he could, to tell me...only I was so locked in grief, I didn't see it. Or the fact that I was unconsciously expecting him to be Solstice.

Gradually, as I rubbed salve into his raw hairless spots and spoon-fed him baby food, we began to bond. He took to hanging out on the stairs with me and burbling away, just as Solstice had. He began sleeping on my bed and doing Kitty Reiki on me, just as she had, albeit a lot more boisterously. But he had a kittenish quality that she had never had, probably because she had been so ill her first year. And he became so affectionate, I couldn't believe I'd ever called him "a cat's cat."

One day around the end of his second month with us, we laughingly watched him spring up, trying to catch the raindrops hitting the breezeway door's long glass panel. And I knew then that Phoenix was more than just a replacement Ruddy – that he was just as magical as his name.

What made him so magical was his ability to love, no holds barred. Once he felt more secure with us, he loved being picked up and held like a baby. He'd simply stand upright on his back legs and place his front paws on my chest: *Hugs now.* It became quite a ritual with him, particularly in the mornings. Didn't matter if he'd just gotten yelled at for crimes against toilet paper and wallpaper border. Didn't matter if I'd just let loose a banshee shriek because he'd just taken a flying leap for me and dug those grappling hooks of his into my side. He'd just stare up at me with those greenish-gold eyes and rear up on his hind feet, ready for lift-off: *Whatever. Hugs now, please.*

You see, Phoenix now had faith – faith that there would always be a pair of loving arms ready to catch him. And if the human attached to those arms sometimes shrieked or scolded...well, Humans Were Like That Sometimes, and You Couldn't Take Them Too Seriously.

No, he wasn't much like Solstice, who had had a tendency to hold back. And yet...One day, Phoenix was sniffing around some take-out I'd just picked up: I thought he was after Marissa's chicken parmagian (which he was very fond of), then realized that he wanted the crust off her peanut-butter-and-chocolate pie. So I broke off a few crumbs, making sure that there was no chocolate stuck to them, and he scarfed them up. Gave him a few more – same thing. Then I remembered.

Solstice had loved peanut butter from the time she was a sickly kitten. Somehow, even with the polyps she had in her throat back then, she could swallow it easily. So I used to give her an occasional teaspoon...one of our many little rituals....And now, as Phoenix practically inhaled those peanut-butter crumbs, my grief finally slipped quietly out the breezeway door. He was the perfect successor to Solstice, after all. I could just see the movie title on an imaginary marquee: "Son of Solstice." All I had ever really needed to do was to make my own leap of faith toward him.

Phoenix has been with us a year-and-a-half and is food-allergy-free now. He is as loving and clueless and spazzy-pawed as ever, and I am still throwing out mutilated toilet-paper rolls. He is still performing acupuncture without a license. But on the plus side, I get hugs from a loving, impetuous Aby every morning, and I've learned a lot about leaping.

THE OFFICE CAT

Hawkeye checks out my bee balm -- and, of course, the birdfeeders near the bee balm -- from my office window. That done to his satisfaction, he leaps onto my desk and stretches his silver-flecked black paws across some of the notes for my novel-in-progress. *I'll just look these over for you,* he assures me, his yellow eyes solemn. *Not to worry.*

And I don't. Phoenix, my lovable harum-scarum Ruddy Abyssinian male and Hawkeye's best bud, would probably chew my notes to bits on general principle. But Hawkeye, aside from kidnapping an occasional woolen glove or leather bookmark that's just asking for it, is fairly respectful of human property.

It's nice having an Office Cat again. I haven't really had one since my beloved Cricket died eight years ago. Cricket started out as a big-eared -- dare I say it? -- cub reporter, sitting on my lap while I typed, her amber eyes lighting up as she *thwapped* one key after another. Or all of them at once. I had more typos than usual in my work, but she seemed immensely satisfied with the results. (Tim and I suspected that she was working on a novel.)

Later, as Cricket matured into a plushy editor-cat, she took to stretching out on the floor near my desk or draping herself over the printer. She was, she indicated gently, willing to brainstorm article and story ideas with me; but she felt that the time had come for me to go it alone as far as the actual writing went. She was, she purred, a Concepts Cat and could I drag that catnip toy a little closer? (The contract for her book must've fallen through.)

After Cricket's death, the other cats wandered in and out of the study, but none really shared her feeling for writing and the tools of the trade. In fact, Topaz, an equal opportunity sprayer, felt that the computer keyboard -- the electronic typewriter -- hell, even my handwritten rough drafts were fair game. I had to Febreze the rough draft of my time-travel novel *Souleiado* in order to finish editing it without gagging.

When we moved to our new house and I set up shop in the small room off the kitchen, I began keeping the door shut. I missed having the cats around while I worked, but it was too difficult keeping Topaz and the other sometime sprayers out. So, except for an occasional invasion by Star -- who naturally refuses to believe that any room could possibly be off limits to *her* -- or a brief stay by a new or sick feline, the study remained cat-less. Until Hawkeye re-assessed the situation, that is.

Hawkeye, who is a Very Serious Guy with his black face and silver markings or "specs" around his eyes, is also a Very Loving, Lovable Guy. But he has, as he has informed us time and again, Issues. His Feelings Get Hurt, he insists, and it takes him awhile to Get Over It.

One of Hawkeye's current Issues involves Phoenix. Now they are, as I've said, best-est buddies: they are both the same age (two) and act like littermates, wrestling and chasing each other through the house. Both are gluttons for attention. But Phoenix, with true Aby flair, takes it a paw-step further: he stands up on his hind legs and, placing his front paws up on my chest, looks beseechingly at me till I pick him up and cuddle him.

Now Hawkeye doesn't care much for being picked up. But he'll come over to me while I'm sitting down and do push-me-pull-yous on my knees while he miaows happily about his day. It's endearing, but it doesn't have the show-stopping quality of Phoenix's paws-up maneuver.

And Hawkeye knew it from the get-go. He would sit there, looking reproachful and pondering the Injustice of Things. After all, he had been here First. He had to one-up Phoenix somehow.

So he began slipping into the study. *Don't mind me -- I just thought I'd come in and make sure the plants are all right.* Then, having given the plants a pep talk, he'd settle down in the window near them and watch the birds at the feeder. *Just doing field research,* he'd assure me.

After awhile, he began moseying over to my desk. He'd lie down and watch me scribbling away. *That description's giving you trouble, huh?* the yellow eyes would say sympathetically, as he put his head down on the paper. *Well, I like it. Very comfortable.*

Once, Phoenix came in with him. *So, this is where you work.* The happy-go-lucky Aby glanced at the plants. *You get eats on the job, too? Cool.*

It's O. K. You could see that Hawkeye was trying to sound casual so that Phoenix didn't start getting ideas about being an Office Cat, too. Some things you don't want to share, even with your best bud.

Hawkeye's a few weeks into the job now, and we both feel good about working together. Of course, Hawkeye can be a surprisingly strict editor sometimes. One night, I was getting ready to close shop -- it was after 10 p. m. -- so I nudged him awake, explaining that I didn't usually work this late.

He opened one eye. *You should. You've been slacking off a bit, and it's starting to show. I've been meaning to mention it.* And he shut the eye tightly.

I sat back down and pulled the rough draft back toward me. You know, he may just be on to something.

KIND HEARTS AND UNEMPLOYED BRAINS

Years ago, Marissa began writing a long funny, imaginative story about a place called Idiot's Paradise. There were many, many characters in this story, and you never knew when you might be woven into it. (One of our friends actually put in a request to play the part of a Russian-sounding Siamese named Sonya.) But the ones who stood out were five friends who saved their homeland from an intellectual takeover. And, of course, Governor Charles D. Topaz, "a Flamepoint Siamese cat goofball with a long nose (like Charles DeGaulle), a kind heart, and an unemployed brain."

Topaz, our 7 ½-year-old Flamepoint Siamese, thinks it's a Very Good Description, and I have to say, I agree with him. It's our four-legged Mr. DeGaulle (Tom, our vet, pointed out the striking resemblance years ago) to a nose. He is lovable and loving and the biggest goofball of a cat I have ever known. About that brain of his...well, Marissa and I have discussed it time and again, and we honestly can't make up our minds whether he's incredibly stupid or freaking brilliant. He certainly acts clueless: he is a repeat offender when it comes to both spraying and picking on our ditzy gray tabby, Merlyn, no matter how many times we have yelled at him or squirted him with the water bottle. Cause and effect simply do not exist in Topaz's universe: he simply wanders through life with all the bumbling innocence of a Red Skelton character.

And yet...he seems to understand tone, if not words, and responds very quickly. Yell "Topaz, tail down!," and the would-be sprayer wraps his red tail round his paws lightning-quick. He is also the inventor of bottle-cap hockey, a very popular game among the younger cats. And he went through a period of making off with any dollar bill that was innocently lying on the table. At first, it was just singles, but then he upped it to fives, which got me wondering: could he really tell the difference between denominations? "If he starts making off with twenties," I remarked to a friend, "I'm going to start worrying." We then speculated that in a previous lifetime, he might have been a high-powered young executive. The fact that he snorted coffee grounds only added a touch of believability to our theory.

When he came to us, Topaz was a big hearty kitten uncannily like Houdini, my first Siamese and the hero of my novel of the same name. Like the feline stowaway of my childhood, he was a throwback to the red tabby part of the Flamepoint equation. In fact, if it hadn't been for that absurdly long nose, Topaz would've been—pardon the pun—a dead ringer for the first Houdini.

He immediately attached himself to the Aby Girls when they appeared on the scene a few months later. He was especially in love with Solstice, the little Ruddy: when she went up to Mary's cattery for A Very Long Honeymoon of three months, poor Topaz went around the house moping for his amber-eyed beloved with the long whiskers. I wasn't sure whom I felt sorrier for—him or Solstice, who was, from Mary's reports, saying She Didn't Like her Fawn Suitor, he was Very Rude, and could she please Come Home now?

Then she *did* come home, and Topaz sulked with right good will, refusing to forgive her for going off with that Fawn Guy, though Solstice swore Nothing Had Happened. He even—I know this sounds like a storyline from one of those Lifetime movies, but cats have their own little soap operas, same as we do—took up with Solstice's mother, Erin, who was staying with us at the time and who was, to put it politely, an infamous type of woman. They would have these down-and-dirty rendezvous alongside or on top of the old furnace. The fact that Topaz was neutered didn't seem to hinder their romance at all.

"Huh," said Tom when he heard the story, "So it really *is* all in the head, after all."

It was a short-lived affair. Erin went back to her cattery. Topaz waited pathetically by the furnace for her: in fact, he waited so long, his creamy white base coat turned decidedly gray. He had lost both his loves. Solstice, on the other hand (paw?), retired from the show-and-breeding circuit due to health reasons and eventually found happiness with Bandit, our big black cat, who loved her for the rest of her days.

The Erin incident and Topaz's behavior in general earned him the name "goofball." He was a comical and, thanks to his spraying, frequently annoying figure. He would wander from room to room at night, making these bleating noises, which led to yet another nickname: "Sheep-Cat." Basically, he became the Clown Prince of Cats, the one we loved but couldn't resist poking fun at. "Hello, Mr. DeGaulle," my brother Marc would say to him. "You have a face for radio."

"Topaz, did you have a thought?" Marissa or I would ask. We had a running joke about Topaz being Terrified of Thoughts because he seemed to need so much reassurance.

"N-nye-ehh!" Topaz would reply, looking down at his long nose of his. He was too worried about not getting attention to take offense.

Then the summer of our discontent came upon us, and the Goofball more than proved himself.

My elderly mother had taken to making hysterical phone calls at all times of the day and night, demanding that I leave my teenage daughter and come over. She was, as we soon learned, suffering from some kind of dementia. Under its sway, the phobias and phantoms she had lived with for so long became all too real, and she wanted me to save her from them.

I went through my days thoroughly sandbagged and began dreading the ringing of the phone. Eventually, we got Mom into adult daycare and we found companions to stay at her house at night and on the weekends. Until that was all in place, however, I found myself running over there two or three times a day. Since I emphatically didn't want Marissa seeing her only surviving grandparent falling apart like so much wet tissue paper, I left her at home alone more than I liked to. I also missed the signs that she was slipping into a severe depression as our lives unraveled more and more.

It was Topaz who came to the rescue. When I couldn't get back to sleep after one of Mom's many phone calls, he hopped up on the bed and curled up next to me, his soft squunky purr soothing me. When Marissa turned from me during the worst of her depression, he rested his triangular Siamese face on my outstretched arm and assured me that he didn't care what They said and that he thought I was Really Quite Nice for a Human...even if I did yell or spritz him with water for spraying. And when Marissa had to be hospitalized, not once but twice, Topaz was there for me, a big squishy Flamepoint teddy-bear of a cat, letting me know that I shouldn't let The Thoughts get the better of me. That *he* would take care of them like so many bugs if they showed themselves....

Mom's dementia is in check now. She has her companions, and the bizarre phone calls have stopped. Marissa has done her dark night of the soul and come out on the other side of it. There are still rough patches, of course, but she is coming back to herself and is creative and engaged with her animals and hobbies once again.

As for Topaz...well, with the heat wave we've been experiencing lately, he has been spending most of the night downstairs with Dawn, one of his "Aby babes." But if I'm having a bad night for whatever reason, he somehow senses it and ambles upstairs to keep me company.

His brain may be unemployed, but his heart is working over-time.

TIKVAH'S KITTEN

The tiny grayish cat with the faint orange splotches in her fur limped through the underbrush, panting. Her paws were sore from running so hard; a thorn pierced though the pad on her front left one. Her usually soft, silky fur was rough and stuck all over with burrs.

She found a hollow -- an old woodchuck hole -- by the base of a tall maple tree and, crawling into it, made herself even smaller. She began washing her sore paw, then stopped, sniffing the warm May air nervously. The fox hadn't followed her, after all. She shivered despite the heat. First, there'd been the shadowy sickness that had sapped the life from her surviving kitten, leaving its gray-striped body lying cold in the long-tall field grasses, and now the fox. Still, she would be safe here. For awhile, anyway. The cat shifted her attention back to her paw, pulling at the thorn with her teeth until she finally worked it loose.

The cat had had a home once, but it was like the shadow of a dream to her now. She'd had a litter shortly after she'd come into her first heat. The humans had gone away before the kittens had even opened their eyes, leaving them all in a cardboard box on the unenclosed front porch without food and water. She'd tried to keep them safe; but her hunting trips had taken her further and further afield. Then, one morning, she'd come back with a chipmunk to find three kittens gone, and the fourth, her little gray girl, scrabbling around in the bushes near the porch, squealing for her, the still-blue eyes large with fear. The coyote stench had been everywhere. She'd grabbed the kitten by the scruff of her neck and taken to the woods beyond the house.

They'd lived there for a long time, chasing each other through the rustling grasses and having wrestling matches, for the mother-cat was little more than a kitten herself. As the kit had grown bigger, the cat had taken her along on hunting trips, showing her how to lie still and gather up strength for the pounce before making a swift, clean kill. And every day, just as the summer sun turned the straw-colored field grasses to shimmering gold, they'd lain near the hollow log that had been their den, catching what breezes they could. Purring, she'd twitched her tail back and forth for her little one to pounce on.

She missed her kitten now. She still had some milk, and her body ached because the little one wasn't there to take it from her.

The hollow by the maple tree made for a good den for the most part. But there were rainy, thundery nights when she had to crouch low and make herself smaller in what was already a very tight space. The cough came on her then: a harsh one that shook her too-thin body like the wind taunting the tree branches in a storm. She couldn't throw that cough off anymore than she could her own skin.

She found an old gray shed near the edge of the woods. The windows were broken, and some of its weathered boards had been ripped away. But it was dry, and the cough didn't claw at her throat so badly. The shed belonged to a thin pale-yellow warrior-cat, however: when he found her there, he drove her away, tearing mouthfuls of fur from her shoulders and back.

Prey was scarce, and the tiger cat grew thin and bedraggled. But she kept moving, the ghost of her kitten moving alongside her like a second self.

Once, she left the shelter of the trees for an open sunny space. Human kittens – boys – were tossing a ball back and forth. She knew boys, she thought. Her humans had had one: he'd always saved bits of his dinner for her and snuck her under the bedcovers with him at night. So she strolled over to the boy who'd been throwing the ball; she mewed happily at him, rubbing her head against his ankles.

He bent over and grabbed her around the middle, squeezing her hard. The cat cried out, all four paws flailing about, her paws clawing the air as he threw her like he had the ball. Harder, even. She managed to land on her feet and scurried off through the underbrush back to the dark safety of the woods.

The cat stayed there for a long time, living off what she could catch. Often, she saw other cats...cats as skinny and big-eyed as herself... prowling among the trees. One white cat with big black splotches all over her coat had lost a front paw in a rabbit trap. Another was blind in one eye from a blow. Most of them had lived with humans at one time or another. Some had been abandoned like the little tiger cat; others had wandered off and forgotten their way back home.

The strays never hunted together. But on cold rainy nights, they huddled together, giving each other what warmth they could. And sometimes on warm sun-glistening days, they'd race through the woods, playing tag. Almost as though they were kittens again.

Near the end of the summer, the tiger cat grew restless enough to follow the ghost-kitten back out into the world beyond the woods. One morning, holding her feathery tail high, she picked her way through the dew-dappled clover till she came to a house with a garden. The garden was brimming over with purply harebells, spicy-sweet thyme, flaunting red bee balm, and orange and yellow poppies with satiny butterfly petals that floated to the ground when she brushed against them. And there was catnip, its dainty bluish-purple blossoms giving off a scent that made her giddy.

She was rubbing against a catnip bush when she sensed she was being watched. A woman stood at the edge of the garden. The cat froze, her muscles tensed for flight. The woman slowly moved closer, then sat down on the grass, holding out her fingers. The cat's tiny rose-colored nose quivered, and she spat. The woman didn't budge. Curious, the cat moved closer and sniffed. Cautiously, she rubbed her head against the outstretched hand. The woman began to stroke her: the cat felt a purr growing inside her for the first time since her kitten's death.

"How about I call you 'Tikvah'?" the woman asked gently. "It means 'hope,' and you look like you could use some." They looked at each other. Then the woman stood up, and Tikvah tensed up again. Crouching among the flowers and herbs, she watched the woman disappear into the house. She nibbled at a stray blade of grass but never took her pale-green owl's eyes away from the door.

Finally, it swung open, and the woman came down the wooden steps with two bowls. She set them down, then parked herself down on the grass, just a few feet away.

Tikvah padded over to the bowls, her nose twitching. One bowl held some broiled hamburger, all broken up into nice chewable bits. She glanced at the woman; then she lowered her head to the dish and began tearing into the meat. Only when that dish was scoured clean did she turn to the bowl of water alongside it.

Her thirst slaked, Tikvah sat up and licked her chops. She studied the woman and found herself remembering her own kittenhood and being held by her mother's humans...securely, their hands bracing her back feet, but not too tightly. The memory tugged at her. But Tikvah did not follow the woman into the house, even though the latter held the door open for her. She lay down, tucking her big front paws under her, and closed her eyes. She would wait.

****

That night, Tikvah crawled under the porch's latticework to sleep. In the morning, the woman was back with fresh food and water. She sat on the steps, drinking her coffee while the cat breakfasted, and talked to her in a low reassuring voice.

Tikvah made her den under the porch. It was fairly safe there, and she could peer out through the latticework without being seen. Whenever the woman came outside to work in the garden or sit at the table and write, Tikvah ran out to greet her and keep her company. Sometimes the woman talked to her, and sometimes she didn't. But Tikvah knew now that she was safe with her.

So, late one afternoon, when the woman held the door open a second time, Tikvah ran up the steps and walked right in. She rubbed against the woman's ankles and mewed, then headed into the kitchen, sniffing the air excitedly. Other cats had lived here, her nose told her, but they had crossed over long ago. The room felt as warm and comfortable as the late afternoon sun on her back. She wrapped her tigery tail elegantly around her paws and glanced up at her new friend with contented kittenish eyes. She began washing her right front paw, satisfied.

That night, she slept at the foot of the woman's bed.

Tikvah spent the next few days exploring the house from cellar to attic. She discovered that the old-fashioned stand-up radiators made excellent perches and that there were lots of good hiding places scattered throughout the house. She had toys now, too – wooden spools, soft bouncy balls, and catnip mice for that she could toss around or chase under the furniture. The woman wouldn't let her go back outside, but she didn't mind that so much. The woods and fields had been frightening places to her, and she pushed the memory of them as far from her as possible as she curled up on the sun-warmed loveseat for a nap.

But she grew lonely for the company of other cats. The woman talked to her, shared food with her, patted and brushed her, and gave her more toys and kitty grass to nibble on. And Tikvah liked being with her. She didn't even mind wearing the silly yellow collar with the brass tag on it. But the woman wasn't much good at cat games. Tikvah would sit by one of the windows, watching the cats who were allowed out and wistfully remembering the times with her kitten and the other strays in the woods. She didn't want to go back outside, no...but it would be nice to have a friend to play with sometimes.

Her ghost-kitten just sat there, looking at her sadly. She curled up next to her mother, but it wasn't the same as having a warm snuggly little kitten body next to you.

The woman took Tikvah to a place where there were other cats sitting on their humans' laps or peering out of their carriers. They looked just as scared of the strange smells and barking as she was, Tikvah thought. They all watched each other curiously through the grille doors of their carriers. But just as she was making eye contact with an Abyssinian, a vet tech came out and took her from the woman.

There was a lonely afternoon in a cage followed by an even lonelier night. Did her new human no longer want her? Tikvah wondered. That was hard to believe; then, again, her first humans had left without warning. She fretted, not even noticing when the tech took her food away. Suddenly, her little daughter was there in the cage with her. True, they couldn't touch noses or snuggle like they once had; but warmth spread through Tikvah's soul, and she somehow felt well enough to sleep.

In the morning, the tech came back and took her to a strange room; she woke up much later back in the cage with her belly shaven and stitched up. The food bowl had mysteriously returned, so Tikvah ate a little and waited for all she was worth.

The next day, the woman came for her. She held Tikvah just right -- close but not too close -- and the little cat felt a purr burbling up inside her. She hadn't purred like that in a long time, not since she and her kitten had lived by the hollow log in the woods. She had to go back in the carrier, of course. But once she stepped out of it into the sunny kitchen, she knew that she was home for good.

She had lost the urge for a mate, but her yearning for her kitten was still with her. Sometimes she pretended that her spongy little soccer balls were kittens and pushed them around with her paws. But after awhile, the pretend magic wore off, and she was left with a slew of grimy pink and yellow soccer balls that had lost most of their black felt spots on their travels about the house. By that point, Tikvah was so bored with them, she just dropped them through the open spaces in the cellar stair risers and forgot about them.

She moped. Even her food lost its appeal. She just poked at it half-heartedly with her paw.

One morning, Tikvah wandered out to the front porch. It was a little enclosed room, just off the living room with lots of windows and a Rose of Sharon in front of it. She hopped up on the wicker table and peered out. The tree with its lush leaves and purply-pink blossoms gave the room a cave-like feel: it was like being outdoors without being outdoors.

She heard the kitchen door open and turned around. The woman came into the living room with the carrier and set it down.

There were little shrill noises coming from the carrier. Tikvah jumped down from the table and hurried over to it, her whiskers quivering. The woman opened the carrier, and a tiny striped female kitten stepped out. Not gray like the little one Tikvah had lost but calico with an orange-and-white mask and slanted pale-green eyes.

Tikvah pushed closer. The kitten opened her mouth in a baby hiss. Tikvah hissed back, just to put the newcomer in her place. Then she headed over to her food bowl. For the first time in days, she ate without being coaxed.

Later, in the middle of the night, a faint cry woke Tikvah. She yawned and looked around her. Nobody there. Curling back up, she was just about to go back to sleep when she heard the cry again. She hopped off the bed. The little newcomer was sitting in the hallway, mewing for her mother and litter mates.

Tikvah went over to her and began nuzzling the velvety tiger head. The kitten didn't hiss at her this time; instead, she snuggled up against the cat's soft belly, trying to nurse. All of Tikvah's mothering instincts flickered back to life. She began bathing the kitten and felt a deep rumble-purr starting up inside herself.

The ghost-kitten sat at the top of the stairs, her eyes a soft, loving shimmer. Then she was gone. Something of her essence would always linger, but she would not come again.

Tikvah gently picked the kitten up by the nape of her neck and carried her up onto the bed. The little one snuggled up close to her new mother. And Tikvah lay there, purring and watching until her kitten fell asleep.

MY OLD MAN

Derv and I were driving to the vets'. My old "orange-and-white guy" was in his carrier on the passenger's seat, of course; but whenever possible, I'd put my fingers through the grid door, and he'd rub his still kittenish face against them. Sometimes I talked to him -- he had an almost human look of understanding -- and sometimes we just listened to the Celtic music on the CD player. There was that feeling of perfect harmony you get when you're hanging out with a very best friend. A kindred spirit. Which, when you get right down to it, I was.

Dervish had just celebrated his 17th birthday. He had come to us as a blue-eyed calendar-cute kitten in the early years of my marriage and had been with us so long, I couldn't recall when I'd stopped thinking of him as a cat. He was simply my friend in a fur suit. He had overseen the training of many younger cats and babysat my son Zeke. He had been the official greeter and "the man of the house" since Tim's death. And now he was a guest columnist with me, a picture of him in his prime (all 22 pounds of it) appearing on cleverkitty.org along with our "Derv & Co." column.

Of course, given his age, he had health issues: arthritis and a megacolon problem. And his temper was no longer quite as even with the younger cats. He preferred to love them -- well, *like* them, at any rate -- from a judicious distance. Which, in his case, meant the topmost perch on one of the cat trees or his "office" -- the lower cabinet of an old bureau in the cellar. One of the doors was missing, making for easy access, and there was a big, fleecy orthopedic blanket inside, just right for an older statescat needing his peace and quiet.

Yes, Derv was feeling his age, all right. But he still occasionally joined me on the breezeway sofa for my morning coffee or hobbled up to the second-floor bedrooms to see what was keeping breakfast.

There was, of course, that whole bumpy terrain of living with an elderly cat that I had to learn the lay of: the nightly medicine wars; the trips to the vet's when the medicine didn't quite do the trick; and the occasional hospitalizations for blockages. Sometimes, given his sluggish colon, I had to coax lamb baby food down him. (The younger cats, especially the Abys, made it clear that they were always ready to assist with this.)

Then, too, he needed help with his grooming now. Combs didn't work: they pulled too hard on him, and elderly cats, like elderly people, have paper-thin skin. I didn't want to stress him out with trips to the groomer, so I did a lot of hand-grooming, carefully working his mats out with my fingers and scissoring them off only when necessary. One summer morning, when I was out running, I spied a pet-grooming van heading up a side road near our house. Talk about answered prayers. I picked up my pace and followed that van...only to find myself stopping short at a place where the road branched off into two longer roads. There was no telling which way the van had taken, and the air was already turning nasty and humid. I sighed mentally and turned back toward home.

Derv and I went back to hand-grooming. He didn't mind. And, to tell the truth, neither did I. It gave us a little more time together. As Derv grew older and I nursed him through various ailments, he became doubly precious to me. Every little thing I did for him -- the hand-grooming, holding a dish of baby food up to him so that he could eat comfortably while resting atop his favorite cat tree, clipping claws that were threatening to become ingrown, even putting Pellitol on his sometimes swollen rectum -- became an important ritual. Loving is, after all, more about the quiet, understated gestures than about the grand sweeping ones: and anything that makes you step outside of yourself brings an ineffable grace with it. The pleasure I felt in seeing Derv perk up and move around like a younger cat, his coat a tad less matted, more than outweighed any squeamishness I initially felt over dealing with some of his health issues.

I had planned a big celebration for Derv's 18th birthday. But the day found him back at the veterinary clinic, getting yet another enema. He came back home, his yellow eyes utterly disgusted: *You humans suck at doing birthdays.* I did try to make it up to him by buying him a nice thick throw for his office; he accepted the gift with grudging, hurt dignity. *That party would've been nice...Nothing big, just a little get-together, some kitty treats and maybe some of that frozen peach yogurt I used to like....*

Derv padded through his 18th year and into his 19th relatively smoothly. True, he was a lot more ornery about his visits to the vets'. Zeke and I suspected that he was miffed over the fact that our Aby-mix Zorro -- who was, after all, only a year younger -- didn't have to go in for his annual vaccinations. Tom wanted to stress Zorro out as little as possible on account of his chronic upper-respiratory problems and age. Derv did not receive the same "Get out of jail free" card, however. *You lucky bastard,* we imagined him saying to his old war buddy. *Sinus problems, my ass.*

The nightly pill wars continued. Cisapride and Enulose for Derv's megacolon condition -- Cosequin for his arthritis. The Enulose came in liquid form and was only slightly less sticky than maple syrup or pine pitch: trying to get the gooey stuff down Derv's throat without coating myself and the entire floor with it required definite hand-eye coordination. Not that pills were necessarily easier. Forget the arthritis: Derv did at pill time and could high-tail it down cellar with the power and the passion of a puma. Failing that, he generally managed to shift the tablet to the side of his mouth and spit it out later.

I stubbornly kept up the battle. After all, he needed those meds, especially the ones to ward off blockages. Finally, Derv decided that the time had come to pull out all the stops. One Saturday night, after pilling him, I sat down on the sofa with a dish of ice cream. Derv sat down, too, on top of his cat tree, just -- excuse the expression -- kitty-corner from me. He fixed a grim eye on me, my old codger-cat, and proceeded to projectile-vomit onto me, the ice cream, and the sofa. Satisfied that he'd hit all three targets -- and taken the ice cream out for all time -- Derv curled up and went to sleep.

Still, what was projectile-vomiting between old friends? Derv and I meandered along together, our affection for each other deepening by the day. We knew each other by heart. Once, the younger cats were acting up more than usual at breakfast time; Derv sat by the doorway, watching them. Then he looked up at me. *Spazzy little bastards, aren't they? Just like I used to be, remember?* And he winked. There was a world of camaraderie in that wink....

One drizzly August morning, I noticed that Derv was having more trouble getting around than usual. Suspecting that he was impacted again, I brought him into the vets'. Tom verified my suspicions and recommended an enema, assuring me that it wouldn't be too much for Derv: it was, after all, a non-invasive procedure.

I picked up Derv right before closing time and fixed up a comfortable place for him in the finished-off part of our basement. I checked on him periodically but basically just let him re-charge his failing batteries. He slept, passed stool, and seemed more himself, moving from one cat condo to another and sometimes even back to his old office.

The next night, I headed downstairs, figuring he could probably benefit from a good clean-up. He hadn't eaten or drunk much of anything either, so I was going to have to help him with that, too. I pulled Derv gently out of the cat condo and gasped. He was rag doll-limp and barely conscious.

Clearly, he had had a stroke and was sinking fast. Since our clinic was closed for the night, that left us with two options: the emergency clinic a town away or another veterinary hospital in another town in the opposite direction. And even if he made it to either place alive, I figured it was a pretty safe bet that the vet on duty would advise me to have him euthanized on account of his advanced age.

I looked down at my orange-and-white guy and made up my mind. If Derv was going to die tonight, he was going to do it in his own home and not surrounded by strangers.

Zeke had joined me by this time. At 15, he had been around enough dying animals to know the signs. He got Derv's fleecy orthopedic blanket out of his office. We lay him down on it, and I covered him with an old bath towel. Zeke cued up Dido's "Life for Rent" CD on his mini-stereo system. It was the right music for the moment -- sweet and sad all at once.

We sat with our old man, thinking that he would die fairly quickly, as he was by now in a coma: he was breathing pretty shallowly, his big bony body jerking at times. But we had reckoned without his heart. The body was failing, but that great strong heart wasn't ready to give up or give out yet.

Zeke sang to him, and I murmured every prayer in Hebrew that I could think of. "I know it's selfish to want to keep him any longer," I choked, "but I can't imagine my life without him." Zeke put his hand on my arm and kept it there awhile; then he went upstairs and came back down in a few minutes with a mug of tea and a badly needed Advil for me.

We stayed with him for roughly two hours. Finally, realizing that nothing might happen for hours, we headed upstairs. I checked on him a few more times, then went to bed. Around 3:30 a.m., I suddenly woke up and made my way down to the cellar. My old friend -- Mighty Derv, as Tim used to call him -- was gone. He had waited for us to leave the room before he'd taken that first paw-step into the Great Beyond.

Numbly, I placed him in a large cooler, putting ice packs around him until my brother Craig and I could bury him later. Then I dragged myself back upstairs, utterly bereft. For 19 years and three months, Derv had presided over our home with the aplomb and geniality of a Buddha-cat; and now, despite the August mugginess, the house felt cold without the warm glow of his presence.

But just as I was drifting off, I saw him near the foot of my bed. He sat there, no longer bony and arthritic but in all the unmatted pumpkin-cat glory of his younger days. And when I ran later in the morning, choking back my sobs, he was with me, his big chest and paws white and glistening in the sunlight as he bounded just ahead of me.

Zeke wrote Derv an elegy. It was so heartfelt and true, I had the closing lines carved onto a memorial stone for him:

Dancing upon the constellations
He will greet us as if nothing's changed
A kittenish smirk inlaid upon his face.

I had no words myself just then, but I planted a white birch tree in our yard, burying a few tufts of orange-and-white fur under it. It became The Derv Tree, and I took extra care of it for his sake. But I still found myself looking for him atop his favorite cat tree every time I walked into the breezeway.

Then, one fall morning, when I was out on yet another run, a young orange-and-white cat came running up to me. Almost as though he'd been waiting for me. His markings were almost identical to Derv's. He rolled over on his side, just as friendly, just as playful as Derv had been at the same age. I squunched down and patted him, feeling, for the first time in weeks, a very bearable lightness of being.

No, I didn't think that this young 'un was my old man reincarnated. Rather, he struck me as being a messenger-cat -- somebody that Derv himself had sent to let me know that all was well with him.

Finally, I rose to my feet and gently shooed him away. "Be careful of the road," I told him. "I don't want you to get hurt."

The cat (his name was Buddy, I learned later, and he belonged to a neighbor) gave me an almost human look of understanding and trotted obligingly across the street. As he did so, a laugh escaped me.

Derv had had -- there is no way to put this delicately -- very big balls and had walked very bow-leggedly. Tim and I had joked that Nature must've had great plans for him. "An incredible race of giant orange-and-white cats," my husband had remarked, facetiously paraphrasing the lines from an old "Twilight Zone" episode. And he had winced mightily when Derv had come back from being neutered -- although he'd been quick to point out to everyone later how "that cat now stood a good two inches higher...."

Well, Buddy was similarly blessed. Of course, his owners would have him neutered when he got a little older. That was the right thing to do. But Nature is a determined lady. Some day, somehow she will succeed in creating her incredible race of giant orange-and-white cats, ready to take over the world. And if they are anywhere near as wise and understanding and loyal as my Derv was, I think we should let them.

THE THREE LIVES OF IRIS

My first life was at the cattery, curled up against my mother's belly with my littermates. We didn't have our masks or points then -- in fact, we didn't look all that much like cats. More like little white rats. But we could purr up a storm. And being Siamese, we found our voices early. I had the loudest miaow, which surprised Teri, our owner, because I was also the shyest of the litter, hanging back and taking my time to get to know the humans who came to look at us.

My brothers and sisters eventually left the cattery for good homes, but Teri kept me. She called me "Lucy" and told me how beautiful I was, "just like a Monet painting." I had no idea what that meant, but I purred for her, anyway. Because I *was* beautiful. My points had come in, and they were a soft blue-gray mixed with cocoa-brown. Very striking against the creamy hydrangea of my base coat. Visitors to the cattery would stop and look twice at me: they were especially taken with my eyes, which were purply-blue and shimmery.

But whenever anyone offered to buy me, Teri always smiled and told him or her, "No." She was keeping me for the cattery, she said: I would go to shows and some day have lots of kittens like my mother.

I kneaded my paws against Teri's shoulder. *Kittens,* I thought. *How nice.*

Then I got sick, and I heard the vet say that there would be no kittens. Ever. The infection had left me barren.

Teri took care of me and loved me as much as she always had. But there were a lot of cats at the cattery. So, when somebody called to inquire about me as a pet for her elderly mother -- the caller had seen my picture somewhere -- Teri gave it some thought. And this time, she said, "Yes."

I had to travel in a special pet carrier on board a plane. The trip was long and frightening, and the place where someone had stowed the carrier was dark and stuffy. I cried for Teri and everything I'd known. After what felt like several of my lives stitched together, the darkness gave way to light. A young-ish woman (the one who had called about me, I guessed) and her child took me from the cargo place and brought me to my new mistress. They also gave me my new name, "Iris"...because, they said, my eyes were the color of an iris flower.

The elderly woman fell in love with me right away. And the son who lived with her fixed up a nice corner for me. But all those hours on the plane had frightened me: I ran upstairs and hid under the woman's bed just in case they were thinking of putting me back on it. Eventually, hungry and tired of hanging out with the dust bunnies, I crept out. My new mistress fussed over me, and her son gave me food and water. When I had finished, I gave myself a good grooming and began checking out my surroundings. The house was small but comfortable. There were lots of little breakables, but I could maneuver around those. These new people were kind, and that was all that mattered.

"Mer-row?" inquired a voice. I turned, and there, sitting in the hallway was Alex, a red tabby Maine Coon cat with a head like a lion's and an affable expression. He touched noses with me. He had been lonely: it had been a long time, he said, since there had been another animal in the house.

Alex was elderly and, for a Maine Coon, very thin. He wasn't feeling quite himself lately, he admitted: he tired easily and had days when he just didn't have that much conversation in him. On his good days, however, he would lie next to me and tell me about his life as a stray before coming here. About Katie, the Springer Spaniel who'd died the year before, and how he used to paw open the kitchen cabinets and knock down cracker and cereal boxes for her to chew on. How she'd bark when people were *leaving* the driveway, not when they were pulling into it. Not the brightest dog in the world, Alex allowed, but a good sort nonetheless.

Then Alex went away in the big blue carrier and didn't come back. Not in his body, at least. But sometimes I would turn a corner, and there he'd be, a magnificent spirit-cat, big and leonine, just as he must've been before I'd known him. He would shimmer in and out, as kindly a presence as he'd always been. Not that the humans could see him, of course. Their vision was too limited.

What they could see, however, was that I was lonely without him. So they brought home a Ruddy Abyssinian kitten to keep me company. Stormy was very playful...always tipping over wastebaskets and rolling around inside them...knocking our mistress' lipsticks off her bureau and chasing them down the stairs like catnip mice. I was delighted. I had always wanted a kitten to mother, and now, in a roundabout unexpected way, I had one.

But, just as unexpectedly, things changed. Or, rather, Stormy did. She grew bigger, more aggressive. Being indoors made her unhappy for some reason, and she would sneak outside whenever she found a door that hadn't been carefully shut. Failing to find one, she would take to the rafters down in the cellar.

When she did emerge from the shadows down there, she acted more like a wildcat than a house cat, hissing and chasing me from room to room. Finally, I took refuge in what had been the son's bedroom. (He had married and gone elsewhere to live, though he was always stopping in to check on us, just as the younger woman and another brother did.) My dishes and litter box were moved in there, and for the next year or so, I rarely left it. Whenever I did, Stormy would seemingly materialize out of nowhere and begin thwacking me with her great Ruddy paws. So it was easier to keep to my little haven.

Looking back, I think that Stormy sensed something was wrong long before I did. Our mistress, who was very old by our reckoning, was growing more confused and frightened. She became as fragile as the figurines she collected, crying and muttering about faces peering in the windows at her. So she began pulling all the shades down, making the house sad and gloomy. But the things she feared were still there in her mind, as real to her as Stormy and I were. Perhaps more.

Something is preying on her brain, I thought, *making her act differently.* Not with me—she was always gentle and loving with me – but definitely with Stormy. Stormy had always been a much more energetic cat, getting into everything she could lay her paws on, and all that wild energy of hers made our mistress more nervous. She took to yelling and swatting at Stormy. Stormy, in her turn, became miserable and acted up even more. Bullying me gave her an outlet for her misery. I didn't like it, of course. But I understood.

Then, one day, we went to the vets' to get our teeth cleaned. The woman's daughter drove us there: she always brought us in for our shots and things. I don't remember much about that day because the vets' helpers gave us something that made us sleepy as newborn kittens.

What I do remember is waking up and finding Stormy in my cage. Only she was softer...a glimmer in time, as it were...and her eyes glowed like leaves in summer sunshine. Gazing into those eyes, I suddenly understood that she had become spirit, just as Alex had. Her heart had stopped during the procedure, she told me; she'd studied her body and decided not to go back into it.

We touched noses gently, and things between us were once again as they'd been in the beginning. She hadn't meant to be unkind: that had been the fear taking hold of her, and she was free of it now. Then she slowly faded away, leaving only a shimmer of light where she'd been sitting.

I did not see Stormy again. Her spirit was, I knew, too wild to haunt houses, especially one where she'd been so unhappy. So I set about re-claiming the house for myself. I could lie on the velveteen loveseat without anybody hissing and chasing me off. I could enjoy being a cat again.

Things were worse with my mistress, though. She kept crying, "I want to go home!," not realizing that she already *was* home. She was still very loving, kissing my head and talking to me constantly. The talk was a ragbag of words, spilling all over the place, but I would sit close to her, purring. It didn't mend her –

there's only so much purring can do – but it did ease her, and the fear would die out of her eyes for a little while, at least.

At night, when I saw her growing tired, I would head toward the stairs and wait for her; slowly, each move jarring her (her back hurt her, and she walked hunched over), she would follow me up to her bedroom, as docile as though she was my kitten. Which, in a way, I suppose she was.

Sometimes she would shut me in a room and forget about me. Fortunately, her children were always stopping by, so one of them would always let me out. And once, she left the outer porch door open: I stepped gingerly out onto the top step and sniffed the air, not sure what I would find. Stormy, I knew, had gone far beyond the trees and tool shed. There had been an overgrown field there, she told me – it had been one of her friendlier more talkative days – filled with tall swishy grasses, blue chicory, butter-and-eggs with their pleated yellow petal caps. And rabbits....But the woman's daughter pulled into the driveway just then. She saw me right away and carried me back into the house. So I never did find out about the world beyond the trees.

The companions started coming after that. Most were kind, though some, the weekend ones, clearly didn't want to be there. My mistress was growing more and more difficult, throwing screaming rages that exhausted everyone, herself most of all. Only Mishka could handle her.

Mishka was the best of the companions, the one who came faithfully every Sunday night and stayed through Friday morning, no matter how bad things got. She was a young woman, but she had a wise and understanding soul. She could coax my mistress into something like calmness and helped me walk her upstairs at night. Mishka would go back downstairs once she was in bed; I would stay and keep watch, just in case those faces showed up in the windows. I never saw them, but my human must've because she would suddenly start crying and screaming. My ears quivering, I would high-tail it downstairs and sit with Mishka in the kitchen until the wailing stopped.

We went on that way for a long time. The rages got worse, and some of the weekend companions didn't come back. I didn't care for the rages either: they made it seem like someone else was there and not the human who had loved me so very much. But, even in my fear, I understood that that screaming witch of a woman wasn't my mistress – that she was buried somewhere deep inside where even I couldn't find her.

Mishka understood that, too, and between the two of us, we took care of her. Perhaps being a cat, I did better. Human vision is, as I've said, extremely limited.

One bitter-cold morning, after Mishka had left for classes, my mistress went outside without her coat on. Some strange people brought her back. They covered her with a thick blanket and asked her what she had been looking for.

I could've told them. She'd been looking for herself. For the person she had been.

My mistress' oldest son and daughter came hurrying in. They talked to her; she turned in their direction but did not seem to see them. She was truly lost now. I wrapped my tail around my paws, and a sorrow I didn't fully understand took hold of me.

The next morning, my mistress went away and didn't come back. Mishka stayed with me that first night and fed me; but she left the next morning, and I never saw her again. I stayed in the living room, waiting and wondering. Then my mistress' daughter and *her* child came and took me away to live with them. I was glad. The house was cold and sad, and having it to myself no longer felt like a good thing.

My new-old humans had other cats. Among them were two other Siamese and three Abyssinians who were kin to Stormy but not as wild. Circe, the Blue Abyssinian, was not quite a year old and had been sickly as a little kitten: she had outgrown it, but she still had a tremendous need to be mothered.

One day, shortly after my arrival, Circe leaped up on the sofa where I was lying. She just *looked* at me. Before I knew it, she was cuddled up against my side, purring. I started purring, too – in fact, you couldn't tell where my purr left off and hers began. And, suddenly, I knew that this was where I belonged.

Gradually, I made friends with the other cats. In a way, it was like being back at the cattery. The woman and her young son did everything they could to make me feel cherished after what I'd been through. The bad memories slipped away. I could just be me...mothering Circe...flirting with Bandit, the big black cat with the gentle eyes and soft miaow...rolling on the breezeway sofa with all four paws in the air like a kitten....

Circe snuggles up close to me now, and I begin washing the top of her head, my purr burbling up in me like a song remembered. This is my last life and my best one: I shall savor it.

CIRCE BEAUCOUP

She looks up at me with those almond-shaped green eyes of hers, and I melt. "Beaucoup," I call softly. "Circe Beaucoup." She hurries over to me, rubs her Blue Aby muzzle against my hand, and playfully nips at my fingers. Then she follows me around the basement as I do my chores, making sure that I don't forget about her. As if I could. She has all the charm of the sorceress we named her for.

The "Beaucoup" came later – just a play on words at first, but it stuck. I like it because it makes her sound like the Bond girl that Phoenix, our Ruddy Aby, thinks she is. But, then, he loved her from the beginning, when she was scrawny and shy and anything but a Bond girl.

She was the odd kitten out at our friend Mary's cattery up in Rochester, New York. You know, the kid hanging out on the edge of the playground, not joining in any Aby games. Even her mother hadn't paid much attention to her. I wasn't 100% sure that she was the right kitten for us, but the only other available kittens were too young to make the flight home.

At the airport, the security people insisted on taking her out of the carrier. Clearly, their expressions said, this was a terrorist suicide-bomber kitten. I stood there, the steam coming out my ears like a cartoon character's. What if she squirmed loose and got stepped on or disappeared into the bowels of the building for good? I swallowed my protests, however, knowing that they wouldn't help Circe or us, any. Finally, they gave her back to us, and we were able to board the plane. There was a plaintive – and lengthy -- commentary from the regulation airline carrier at our feet, but the flight itself was uneventful.

Circe surprised us by settling in almost immediately. A good part of that was due, of course, to the fact that Phoenix fell head-over-paws in love with her within a half-hour of her coming through the door. He played Kitty Tai Chi with her, bathed her, and even tried to mate with her...forgetting that he had been neutered a few years earlier. Fortunately for his ego, Circe was too young to know the difference and comment.

The other cats more or less accepted her. Rory, our older Blue Aby, became a sort of big sister to Circe. Then Star, our Sealpoint Siamese, decided to adopt the newcomer. Star, who had gone to the Joan Crawford School of Mothering, would go from lovingly grooming her new charge to biting the tender Abyssinian ears. Circe was in ecstasy, though. She had finally found a mom...an imperfect, unpredictable one, yes, but light-years better than her real one...and she was loved.

Loved, but not healthy. She was having constant and sometimes bloody diarrhea and losing what precious little weight she had. I fed Circe a special diet, gave her meds and Reiki, and spent some wakeful nights over her. We'd had a bad spell eight or nine years earlier, when we'd lost several kittens, and their thin sad-eyed little ghosts came back to haunt me now.

I brought her into the veterinary clinic. Fritz, one of our vets, looked Circe over and didn't seem unduly worried. He thought she might have a low-grade fever or a slight complication from her recent spay surgery. "Try Clavamox," he advised genially. I swallowed a sigh, gathered up our kitten and her antibiotic, and hoped he was right.

And he was. After a few days of Clavamox, Circe turned the corner: the bloody diarrhea stopped, and she began putting on weight. She no longer resembled the little waif from the cattery. She had Phoenix, a way better cat family, and Fitz-dog, a Beanie Baby Irish setter that she dragged happily around the house. From where she lay, kicking Fitz-dog into shapeless submission, it was a Cinderella story come true. We imagined her writing gloating letters to the snotty step-cats back in Rochester.

But, as one Blue Aby waxed big and sleek, another waned, her saucer eyes losing their light and her coat its brushed-velvet feel. We lost Rory to kidney failure that November. Hanging in our upstairs hallway is a photo taken just a few months before her death: in it, Rory is gently bathing Circe, who has the most beatific expression on her face. There is a feeling of spiritual or psychic transference going on. A passing of the catnip mouse, as it were....

Did Circe miss her? Hard to say. For what it's worth, however, she grew more and more like Rory. She showed the same moxie, the same playful friendliness. She even began copying some of her adopted sister's habits. For instance, I'd be sifting the litter boxes in the cellar, and Circe would suddenly appear out of nowhere, select a newly-sifted litter box near me, and squat down in it. *Stay right where you are,* the green eyes seemed to say. *I'll be done in just a few.*

I had to laugh. It was so very Rory.

Circe began to run a little wild, almost as though she was making up for all that time she'd lost being sick. People's shoulders became bridges for her to leap up on without warning to get from one end of the counter to another. They also, Circe indicated, made great strategic positions to wage war on the hanging plants from. She was very much the calamity kitten. Somehow she managed to almost choke herself on her safety collar, and I had to position a tall cat tree by a shelf in the basement after she almost strung herself up on the clothesline near said shelf.

What she needed was a playmate. Phoenix couldn't keep up with her manic hummingbird energy, much as he loved her. Star's maternal devotion didn't go that far, thank you. Iris, my mom's gentle Siamese, who had just come to live us, adored Circe but was a sedate, matronly sort of cat, well past her running-with-kittens days.

Enter Phoebe.

Phoebe was a friendly, fluffy charcoal-gray stray cat who followed me into a local antiques shop one just-above-zero February day. She had had kittens, the woman at the shop told me – Phoebe was a regular there -- but no one knew what had happened to them. Coyoted, probably. I brought her to our veterinary clinic; she stayed there for a few weeks and then came to our house. We would, we told ourselves, foster her from there. Phoebe, however, had Other Ideas.

Within two days of her arrival, she and Circe were chasing each other up and down cat trees. They had bonded. Circe was over-joyed, and, looking at them, I knew I didn't have the heart to separate them.

They became the Thelma and Louise of our cats. One morning, I was sitting on the breezeway couch with my coffee: from there, I could see the high-speed chase going on in the hallway. Circe whipped by for the umpteenth time. Phoebe, coming up from the cellar, suddenly reared up wild-mustang-style; she somehow got enough momentum going to actually go after her buddy *on her hind legs*, holding her front paws straight out in front of her and looking like a benevolent werewolf.

I stared. I couldn't possibly have seen that, could I? I asked my coffee mug. But I had. Hadn't I?

Armed with a new best buddy, Circe really came into her own. She had charm, she had It, as they used to say. Had she been human, she would've been the girl who got all the valentines, the one who had a sea of friend requests to wade through on Facebook. All the male cats were ga-ga over her, not just Phoenix. I mentioned this to Tom during one of Circe's check-ups.

"So, they all suck in their stomachs and stick out their chests?" he dead-panned.

"Yep. That's pretty much it," I dead-panned back.

But it wasn't. Not really. Circe, who had been so forlorn and all-by-herself-ish back at the cattery, turned out to be a relationships girl. Whatever she got, she gave back 100%. And she was loyal right down to her Aby bones. When Iris was dying of cancer, Circe was the only cat who *didn't* avoid her. In fact, she slept curled up by her second Siamese mama's side the night before Iris made her last trip to the vets'.

Circe is four now. She and Phoenix are still an item: when he came back from an overnight stay at the vets' last summer, she hopped up to greet him, and he rubbed his head happily against hers. Sometimes I wander into the spare room and see two lumps under the quilt: I lift the material, and two Aby faces, one Ruddy, one Blue, peer drowsily up at me. *Would you mind? We're on a date,* they gently reprove me, and I lower the quilt. Their romance is definitely here to stay.

She still hangs with Phoebe, too. After all, you have to have a BFF to discuss your boyfriend with. She's friends with all the younger cats and has even made an effort to befriend Sushi, a former stray with a backpack full of issues.

Still, there are some changes that Circe has to reckon with. At 15, Mama Star is in the early stages of kidney disease and a little more temperamental than usual. One morning, Circe hopped up on the bed for their usual snuggle: Star wasn't feeling particularly gracious or maternal and snapped at her foster daughter. Circe stared back, confused and a tad hurt. Then Mama Star had one of her inexplicable changes of heart and began washing her. Circe settled back, closing her eyes blissfully. She had not only forgiven but forgotten; she had somehow tapped into her adopted mom's best side, and that was the side Star was showing her now.

Like I said, that Aby has a genius for friendship.

LOVE, GRIEF & LETTING YOUR HEART OFF THE LEASH

(This is Circe's take on things. It originally appeared on The Conscious Cat blog on February 2, 2012.)

Phoebe was going to write this guest post. But she knew that I had a story to tell, so she said I could take her turn. She's a good friend. And it's a good story, too...one with happy parts...sad parts...and the kind of ending I've heard humans call "bittersweet."

I came from a cattery way up north. The woman there was good to me, but the other Abys weren't. They shunned me because I was little and sickly. Even my own mother took no notice of me. So I just sat there, wistfully watching the other kittens tumble and wrestle with each other and wondering what it would be like to really feel like I belonged somewhere.

Then I came here. Phoenix, a handsome Ruddy Aby, greeted me right away and started showing me around the house. He told me that I was beautiful – he was a very friendly up-front sort of cat – and that I should forget all about what the Abys back at the cattery had said. I was his girl now, and he'd take care of me. And he did. We did Kitty Tai Chi together...watched the birds outside the window together...snuggled under the spare-room quilt together....It was The Best.

A few trips to the vets' and a lot of Clavamox later, I began putting on weight. My coat got glossier, too. Blue roan, they called my coloring. *Very* stylish, I thought.

I also got a new mom. Two new moms, actually. First one was Star, an older Sealpoint Siamese. The second was Iris, a matronly Blue-cream-tortoiseshell point Siamese. Iris was the gentler of the two; Star sometimes got annoyed for no reason and nipped or swatted me about the ears. But she was, on the whole, so much more loving than my real mom, I kinda overlooked those times.

And there was Phoebe, whom some of you have already met. She joined the household that winter, and we became best friends right away. We still are.

Yep, it was a whole different world than the one I'd been born into, and I purred myself silly about it. But I learned something about myself, too. I learned that I was really good at loving.

Loving means that you let your heart go around without a leash on. (Not that I've ever worn one, of course. But I've seen dogs on leashes at the vets'.) Your heart goes bounding up to someone, the way Phoenix came bounding up to me the night I arrived. You belong, without knowing how you belong. You just do. It's an incredible feeling.

But loving someone can also hurt your heart, as I discovered when Iris died. Iris had always been plump for a Siamese: well, she began losing her appetite, and one day, she just wasn't plump anymore. The Older Human kept bringing her to the vets and trying to feed her with this little plastic tube. Of course, we cats knew what our human and the vet didn't: there was a cancer growing inside Iris. We could smell it. The other cats avoided her. But I stayed, remembering. I even slept next to her the night before she made her last trip to the vets'.

I missed Iris, but I still had Phoenix. And Phoebe. And Star.

About a year ago, Star's kidneys began to go bad. The Older Human tweaked our diets, and she perked up. Oh, she snapped more often; and I'd always pull back, kinda hurt and puzzled. Then she'd start washing me again, loving as ever, and I'd settle back against her, happy again. It had, after all, been the illness talking, not my Mama Star.

But the illness grew stronger with time, and the flame inside her grew dimmer. One afternoon, the Older Human put Star into the carrier: I ran over and gently poked my paw through the door's grille. Phoenix came over and washed the top of my head reassuringly. *It's just a check-up,* he told me. *She'll be back.*

And she was. I hopped right into that carrier before Star even had a chance to stretch a paw. We stayed there, nestled together for a long, long time.

She made her last trip to the vets' a few weeks later. I was beside myself. I knew that Star lived on in spirit – we cats are very attuned to that – but I missed her physical presence. Because of my lonely kittenhood at the cattery, I had a greater craving for touch than the other cats did. I got mopey and wandered around the cattery, a little blue-roan ghost-cat.

My friend Sushi helped. Now, she isn't the most socialized cat out there. She just kinda hangs our on her shelf in the cellar and eats. Doesn't even play with the catnip toys that the Older Human brings her. We visit some, and she's always glad to see me. But we don't run races, play poke-paw, or do Kitty Tai Chi together.

Then, one night, she really surprised the whiskers off me. I jumped up on her shelf for a visit, and she began washing my head.

Something warm and glowing filled me, and I could feel a purr starting up in me again...burbling through me like the Older Human's coffeepot. I turned about and leaned into Sushi's blue-tortie fur. Just like I used to with Star. It wasn't the same, but it was close. And at that moment, close was more than enough.

PHOEBE'S MAGIC

The cat was sitting on the steps of the antiques shop when I pulled into the tiny parking lot. Almost as though she'd been waiting for me. Charcoal-gray and fluffy with a wonderful feather boa of a tail, she might've stepped right off the lid of a Victorian chocolates box. She was, I thought as I got out of the car, the perfect antiques store cat.

I closed the door softly so that I wouldn't startle her and peered up at the lavender sign with its elegant black lettering:

Phoebe's.

Well, now, that was different. No *Grandmother's Attic* or *Roses of Yesteryear*. Just *Phoebe's*. Funny how I'd never noticed it before. I drove by here all the time.

I walked up the steps. "Hello here, kitty," I murmured, reaching down to pat her. She sniffed my finger tips – she must've smelled our cats, Circe and Iris – and then ever-so-graciously rubbed her muzzle against them. "*Brr-ff-t?*" she asked.

"*Brr-ff-t,*" I replied. I opened the shop's door. "Coming in?"

"*Skraw-ww,*" she said and padded in. I followed.

The room was a comfortable jumble of carnival and Czech glass, hand-painted china, kerosene lamps, sun catchers, and jar upon jar filled with shells, marbles, and sea glass or "mermaid's tears." There was a slightly musty smell from the old books that had taken over the wall to the east. And just to the left of that, humming and not completely hidden behind her cluttered wooden counter, was a tall, thin woman with thick white hair and a fine-boned face.

The cat jumped up on the counter. "*Mrr-rtt,*" she said, bumping her face against the hand that stretched out to welcome her.

"Well, hello, Phoebe," the woman said. "Have you brought company?"

I stared. "You're not Phoebe?"

"No," she laughed, gently ruffling her friend's fur. "But Phoebe here showed up around the time my partner and I were getting ready to open up the shop. We were feeling kinda tired and irritable from all the work we'd been doing and couldn't come up with a name we both liked. And then Phoebe appeared out of nowhere. It was such a bitter-cold day, we let her in and gave her bits of our bag lunches.

"She made these pretty little noises, just like birdsong they were, and we just looked at each other and said, 'Phoebe.' And then one of us – I forget who – said, 'Let's call the store *Phoebe's*, too -- it's kinda unexpected-like.'" Maribel scritched the cat's ears. "Phoebe comes to visit pretty regular now and sometimes even brings her kittens with her, don't you, Phoebe?"

"*Mr-rt*," Phoebe answered. She started pawing thoughtfully through a basket overflowing with odds and ends of jewelry. She picked up a wooden bracelet – black with a delicate silvery-gray design painted on it – in her mouth and trotted over to where I stood. She dropped the bangle down on the counter and looked at me.

Maribel laughed again. "Phoebe's very playful and likes retrieving. She probably wants you to throw it for her. Or maybe" – the older woman gave me a look a lot like Phoebe's – "maybe she thinks you should have it."

"Huh?'

"She does that sometimes. She seems to have this knack for knowing what people need, even before they know it themselves."

Phoebe pushed the bracelet up against my hand. I laughed, too, this time. "O. K., Phoebe, you win."

"Wait a sec – I think there's another one that goes with it." Maribel began rummaging through the basket herself. "Aha! Here it is!" She held up another black wooden bracelet with a slightly different design and handed it to me.

I turned the bracelets this way and that way, studying them carefully. "They certainly are striking," I said, placing them back down on the counter. "I've never seen anything like them." I pulled out my wallet and took out a few bills. "How much do I owe you?"

Before Maribel could reply, Phoebe trotted over and pawed at the bills. Grinning, I held out a single: she took it gently in her mouth, just as she had the bracelet, and brought it over to Maribel.

"She does that a lot," the shop owner chuckled. "Ones – fives – tens. Never seen her take a twenty yet, but she did make off with someone's checkbook once. Didn't get very far with it, but she clearly had plans."

She took the single from Phoebe and smiled: in that smile, I saw all the warmth and lightness of an early June morning. "You know, I think Phoebe's right about these bracelets. A dollar's a fair enough price for them. They don't really have all that much value: they're just pretty painted things that were part of this old lady's estate. A girl she'd gone to school with had given them to her, her niece told me."

"Thank you," I murmured. "And thank you, too, Phoebe." The pretty little cat came over and, standing up on her hind legs, put her front paws on my chest and nuzzled the side of my face. Then she sat down on her furry haunches and began making those bird-like sounds at me. Clearly, she was well-named.

"Phoebe likes you," Maribel said. "You'll have to come back and meet her kittens. And Kitty Linda."

"Kitty Linda?"

"My partner. She rescues and places stray cats on the side. She's been trying to round up Phoebe and her brood for awhile now. Phoebe by herself wouldn't be a problem – she must've been a house cat at one time, you can see how she is with folks. But her kittens are pretty wild and uncatchable. Still, they come in with her sometimes – their curiosity gets the better of them, I guess."

Mindful of the time – I had to be picking my daughter, Ariel, up from drama rehearsal soon – I said my good-byes and promised to come again. And since between them, Maribel and Phoebe had practically given me the bracelets, I bought a book by way of a thank-you. But it wasn't just a matter of manners. The

book was one I'd been searching for for years: *The 13th Is Magic.*
A teacher of mine had read it to us back in grade school, and its
story had always stayed with me somehow. And now it was mine.
Just like that.

Ariel loved the bracelets. Turned out, they were exactly what
she needed to set off the costume she was wearing in the
historical play that the drama club was putting on.

Funny how often I found myself stopping at the shop after
that. Lynxie, our car, just seemed to know her way there, her
engine purring almost as loudly as Phoebe herself. Maribel would
be waiting, ready with a cup of herbal tea and good conversation.
Sometimes Kitty Linda was there, too — being younger, she did
most of the legwork, going to the estate sales and auctions — and
it was a regular two-part harmony the way they worked together.

Phoebe, of course, always put in an appearance, sometimes
bringing her three kittens with her. Maribel was right about their
being wild: at first, they'd puff out their fuzzy comma-like tails
and spit demonically if I even put a hand out to them. But once I
gave up trying, it all seemed to come more easily, and they'd play
near me, wrestling with each other in wildcat glee.

Sometimes Phoebe would join in, too. After all, she was a
young mother, probably not much more than a year-and-a-half-
old and had plenty of playfulness in her. The kittens would be
chasing each other through the aisles, and Phoebe would lie in
wait, her plumy tail twitching: then, just as soon as she judged the
moment right, she'd give chase. Once or twice, she reared up and
got so much momentum going, she actually went stalking after
them...looking so much like a little gray werewolf, Maribel, Kitty
Linda, and I laughed till our sides ached.

But, then, Phoebe was magical. And so was the shop. Like
Phoebe, it seemed to know what I needed even before I knew it
myself. I was always stumbling across the unexpected there. More
out-of-print books that I'd given up hope of ever finding. Plates
that completed a set my late mother had given me years before.
Pinking shears...which came in handy for a home-economics
project Ariel had to do. Even a sampler that I had done as a kid,

with its weird muddle of colors (I'd refused to follow directions) and my initials squiggled in the lower right-hand corner.

"I can't charge you for your own sampler," Maribel laughed, putting her hand up in protest when I took my wallet out.

I put it back in my purse and stared at the gaudy embroidery. "I wonder how it got here," I marveled. "Mom and I must've put it one of our tag sales, but I never would've expected it to come back to me full-circle like this."

My friend shrugged. "You know how it is around here by now, Fey. Things just kinda find their way where they're supposed to be."

"Magic happens," agreed kitty Linda, who had just walked in the a Nantucket basket from an estate sale in one hand and a carrier with a rescued stray cat in the other.

But even magic can't keep sadness out entirely. One day, I came in to find Phoebe wandering around, her green eyes utterly bereft. Even her usually perky plumy tail drooped. She made none of her talky trilling noises, only this soft little cry that held all the sadness of the world in it.

"Her kittens are gone," Kitty Linda sighed, pushing her thick hair out of her face. "A coyote probably got them."

"Poor little mom-cat," Maribel said sadly.

"I'd bring her home with me," Kitty Linda continued. "But I've already got eight cats, not counting this new one I'm fostering."

"I can't either." I shook my head. "Circe's young and would probably love having a cat closer to her own age to play with. But Iris is twelve and pretty set in her ways....I don't think she'd take to a newcomer."

"Probably not," Maribel agreed, her voice suddenly sounding very old and tired. "We must do what we can for her."

So we spent the next few weeks doing what we could to ease Phoebe's sadness. Even Ariel, who had fallen in love with both the cat and the shop, got in on the act during the weekends. Catnip toy-tossing, crunchy treats, endless petting and scritching...all this and more we did for Phoebe. And being an exceptionally mannerly cat, she was very appreciative, rubbing against us and burbling her thanks. I don't think she ever completely forgot her kittens. But cats live in the present, and Phoebe was not so sunk in sorrow that she couldn't appreciate a good catnip mouse.

Somehow, with all this going on, Kitty Linda, Ariel, and I missed the fact that Maribel herself was sick. Very sick. Suddenly, Kitty Linda was at the shop all the time, and Phoebe sat on the counter, a watchful little shadow-cat.

"She knows," Kitty Linda said, scritching Phoebe's face. Phoebe nuzzled her hand in return...but that was, as I've said, because she was an exceptionally mannerly cat. Clearly, her heart wasn't in it, any more than ours were in what we were doing. "They say cats and dogs can smell cancer. Do you think that's true?"

"I don't know." We had just lost Iris, our Siamese, to cancer the week before. "It makes sense, I guess – they pick up on so many things that we don't."

The end came much more quickly than we'd expected. Mercifully so for Maribel. We knew that and were glad for her sake, sorry for our own. A week after the funeral, I stopped by the shop to check on things. I found Kitty Linda untangling some antique necklaces. Phoebe sat by her on the counter, head tilted to the side and one gray paw poking at a stray chain.

I patted Phoebe. "How're you doing?"

Kitty Linda set aside the cat's-cradle of necklaces and sighed. "It feels strange being here without her. She was like a second mom to me. And things are kinda slow right now. But I'm going to see if I can keep *Phoebe's* going. Maribel would've wanted that, I know."

"I'm glad," I said softly. "I would hate to think of its not being here." I glanced at the cat, who was still playing with the necklace. "What about Phoebe herself?"

Phoebe let go of her catch and looked up.

"I don't know," Kitty Linda answered. "I do worry about her with the heavy traffic and all. And, of course, the winter'll be coming soon – I hate to think of her out in the cold and snow. She could stay in the shop, but what if the driving's bad and I can't get out to feed her?"

I stood there, not knowing what to say.

Phoebe took matters into her own paws. She strolled over to me and stood up on her hind legs, putting her front paws on my chest, just as she had that first day. I gazed into those green eyes, and, all at once, I knew.

"She's coming home with me," I said. I picked her up, and she rested in my arms, easy as a baby. She'd never let anyone except Maribel hold her before. "*Mrr-rtt-t*," she told me, patting my face with her paw. I laughed and tried to hold her the way I'd seen Maribel do it – not too loosely but not too tightly either. Phoebe blinked and purred approvingly.

Circe would be glad, I thought, lulled by the warm burbling sound. She had been missing her friend Iris terribly. And so, I suddenly realized, had we. Phoebe, as usual, knew what folks needed, even when they didn't.